FROM STRAY DOG TO
WORLD WAR I HERO

FROM STRAY DOG TO WORLD WAR I HERO

*The Paris Terrier Who Joined
the First Division*

GRANT HAYTER-MENZIES

Foreword by Pen Farthing

Introduction by Paul E. Funk II

POTOMAC BOOKS
An imprint of the University of Nebraska Press

All rights reserved. Potomac
Books is an imprint of the
University of Nebraska Press.
Manufactured in the United
States of America.

Library of Congress
Cataloging-in-Publication Data
Hayter-Menzies, Grant, 1964–
From stray dog to World War I hero:
the Paris terrier who joined the First
Division / Grant Hayter-Menzies;
foreword by Pen Farthing;
introduction by Paul E. Funk II.
    pages   cm
Includes bibliographical
references and index.
ISBN 978-1-61234-721-9 (cloth: alk. paper)
ISBN 978-1-61234-792-9 (epub)
ISBN 978-1-61234-793-6 (mobi)
ISBN 978-1-61234-794-3 (pdf)
1. Rags (Dog) 2. World War, 1914–1918—
Biography. 3. Dogs—War use—United
States—History—20th century.
4. Working dogs—United States—
Biography. 5. United States. Army.
Infantry Division, 1st. I. Title.
D639.D6H39 2015
940.4'12730929—dc23
2015024887

Set in Lyon by M. Scheer.
Designed by N. Putens.

To all the animals, past and present, who serve human ends and, though they have no choice, serve faithfully.

To Freddie, whose rescue and adoption changed your life and the lives of your dads. You are *our* hero.

In grateful memory of b j Altschul

Since the beginning of history, animals have shared the hardships of fighting men, and Rags was an outstanding example of devotion. He was a real soldier dog.

—MAJ. GEN. FRANK PARKER (1872–1947),
New York Times, March 22, 1936

CONTENTS

ILLUSTRATIONS

FOREWORD

Pen Farthing

There is no stronger bond than that between a man and his dog.

Any dog owner will tell you of the loyalty and companionship shown by his or her canine counterpart. Throughout history there have been many tales of the courageous and brave acts of selfless hounds to protect their human companions—the guide dog leading its owner out of the burning World Trade Center, the faithful pet leaping into the river to save its family's child from drowning, and the sniffer dog, trained to seek out the treacherously planted IEDs in Iraq or Afghanistan, saving a weary soldier from horrific injuries. And the true story of Rags is no different. The fact that almost one hundred years on we are still talking about a Border terrier and his exploits is testament enough to his legacy.

Although lovingly cared for and with the best protection that could be offered by the soldiers of the First Division, Rags had no choice but to be in the thick of the battle alongside his human owners. Rags provided the companionship expected of a dog and then later delivered messages across the dangerous front lines and identified damage to the communication chain in true canine fashion, with a wagging tail and an eagerness to please.

As a former Royal Marine who served in both Iraq and Afghanistan, I know firsthand the feelings of vulnerability from the threat of the unknown as we served on the front lines. Although it is difficult to describe, there is something reassuring about having a trusted canine by your side. Just as the soldiers of a century ago found comfort with their trusted canine companion Rags as the shells and small-arms fire raked around them on the battlefield, so did I with an Afghan stray called Nowzad. In the lull of a battle, I would often find my young Royal Marines slipping Nowzad biscuits or just spending time in the dog's company. To those weary lads it was a few brief seconds of normality during the stress of war when they could be whisked away to a place of abstract safety.

To some I guess it will seem inconceivable that a dog could bring any comfort to hardened battle veterans such as the soldiers of the First Division, but Rags did. He was the true embodiment of "man's best friend."

As you will read in this marvelous book, Rags was closely associated with three prominent soldiers during his long, colorful life. But I would wager that many more soldiers of the First Division would have laid claim to that dog. Rags was the unit's mascot, and he probably associated with every soldier in it.

The concept of animals in war is not new, but now, as it should, the general public is remembering the service and dedication given by the elephants, camels, goats, donkeys, mules, horses, carrier pigeons, and of course dogs during man's many conflicts, just as soldiers who took part in those campaigns already do. Every year on Remembrance Sunday in London, we pay fitting tribute to those animals who had no choice but to be involved in our conflicts at the specially built Animals in War memorial in Hyde Park. Now I personally will add another name to the list I silently remember: Rags.

INTRODUCTION

Paul E. Funk II

The cost of war has always been measured in lives lost, as well as in the economic impact to the greater society. However, movies such as *War Horse* enlighten us to the tight bond formed between human and animal as they both suffer the ravages of war together. History has seen this reflected since the beginning of time. Hannibal and his elephants, armies of horse-mounted cavalrymen, mine-sniffing dolphins, and even "man's best friend," the soldier dog, are all examples of animals joined with humans in conflict.

The military working dog is another example that demonstrates how dogs and their handlers become inseparable over time. During the wars in Iraq and Afghanistan, American society has been increasingly exposed to how tight this bond really is. A dog lies next to the casket of her handler, unwilling to leave, another lies guarding his handler in an airport, not allowing anybody to disturb his slumbering master. Rags is the perfect example of a dog who dedicated much of his life to the service of the United States, specifically by adding to the annals of the First Infantry Division's storied history. Rags epitomized many of the army's core values by displaying a strong sense of loyalty, duty, self-less service, honor, and personal courage on a daily basis. He is rightly recognized in this book for his numerous sacrifices and is deserving of recognition.

Rags, who served his country with distinction, took part in many battles that remain an essential part of the First Infantry Division's history. The names of Soissons, Saint-Mihiel, and Meuse-Argonne ring as clearly today as they did in World War I. The author is correct in stating that Rags belongs to the entire First Division. I would add that he belongs to the entire nation.

ACKNOWLEDGMENTS

Writing the life of an animal is a bit like writing the life of a medieval saint, one who left no records, only remembered actions. The spirit the writer attempts to conjure is remote, almost inaccessible, undefined except insofar as he made an impression on those around him whose later memories of him, handed on to successive admirers, become narrowed and diffused with emotion, as exaggerated in some areas as understated in others.

I have tried to tell Rags's story through the eyes and hearts of those who knew him. I have also followed my own memories of the animals it has been my privilege to know and love over the course of my life. I bring this perspective because of my parents. To this book I bring their own love of animals, especially dogs, their encouragement and guidance, from my infancy, in appreciation and care for them, and their respect for the mutts of this world. And if I have made Rags live again for those who may have never heard of him, it is because in my family there are generations of beloved companion animals, dozens of faces with names and hearts and souls, the memory of whom is still very much alive. My parents, and our animal family, taught me that there are no little hearts, no little lives. I thank them and love them with all of mine.

Without Rags's human family, I could never have told his story. Jay and Judy Butkus, the Hon. Raymond G. H. Seitz, Helen Seitz, Teresa Thompson, and Emily Butkus (and the spirits of Puddin, sandy paw prints and all, and Jack, who has joined her), thank you all for allowing me into your lives to tell the story of the dog who, for you, has never died. Heartfelt thanks also to Claudia Kemmerer Ruibal, Charles Kemmerer, Warren G. Cox, Grace Ebneter, and Ella Cox for giving me the opportunity to tell the story of your ancestor, First Sgt. George Earl

Hickman of the Sixteenth Infantry, and to restore him to the context of Rags's own life story, from his rescue in 1918 to his rediscovery in New York City in 1925, and beyond.

I could never have outlined the story of Aspin Hill Memorial Park, where Rags and hundreds of other beloved animals lie, without the research and encouragement of the late b j Altschul. One of her last emails to me, a month before her death, was a single line about Rags: "I love that wonderful little dog." I am grateful she knew that this book was in the process of being born. And I am grateful to have met Cori, the dog b j rescued, who in turn rescued and protected her.

I owe special acknowledgment to my aunt, Posie Sutton-Lieder, a woman for whom courage and conviction run deeply, not simply as granddaughter of World War I naval hero Rear Adm. Byron E. McCand-less but also because she had a formidable example in her grandmother Mimi Kitson McCandless. A lady of refinement and fearlessness, Mimi thought nothing of standing between a donkey and its whip-wielding tormentor on the streets of 1920s Istanbul or of purchasing on the spot ponies being abused at carnivals. Dear Posie, you carry that passionate compassion through your own life and in everything you do. Thank you.

My siblings, Sean W. Menzies and Ronda L. Menzies, know all that is in my heart, because we share the same love for the animals who give our lives color, emotion, purpose, and inspiration. Thank you for your support, your encouragement, and your love.

My thanks to Bill Luce, mentor and friend for over three decades, who gave me the treasures of music, books, and the belief that as a writer I would always have something to say that was worth reading. Above all, his love for animals has been an inspiration and a standard to live up to.

John and Elizabeth Holland, you spent the better part of a glorious September day indoors just to capture for this book a photograph of Rags's "pawtograph" in the Imperial War Museum in London. Rags and his biographer salute you!

Thank you, Sarah Singleton, Pen Farthing, Bill Wynne, and Joel Eugenides for sharing with me the stories of the dogs you love and for showing me something of what Rags inspired in all who knew him.

Special thanks to Cris Bombaugh, Dr. Gay Bradshaw, Philippa

Campsie, Adam J. Carey, Joanna Church, Donald Coates, Dr. Stanley Coren, Dr. Pamela Kyle Crossley, Dr. Dennis Cunniff, Mark Derr, Major General Paul E. Funk II, Maria Goodavage, Bruce Guthrie, Kristin von Kreisler, Edward Lengel, Dr. Jeffrey Moussaieff Masson, James Mayhew (and the memory of Henry), Monica Mayse, Gary Mead, Ingrid Newkirk, Gail Patten (and the memory of Alistair), Lisa Rogak, Jane Rosen, Kristen Elias Rowley, Michael Shaver, Aimee Stoltz, Charles P. Summerall IV, and Mary Elizabeth Thurston.

The loving encouragement and untiring research assistance of Les Hayter made the writing of this book possible, as did Freddie, just by being who he is. I treasure you both (and the memory of Jessie) more than I can say.

There are still many Ragses in our world—on streets, in puppy mills, in shelters—waiting for you to find them. Please give them a chance to be your hero.

PROLOGUE
Aspin Hill, March 1936

At the advent of spring, they are burying an old soldier.

Born in France, he died in a suburb of the U.S. capital in the deep winter of his days.

From the vantage point of this March afternoon in 1936, the war in which he had fought eighteen years earlier seems both an immeasurably long time ago and reassuringly distant, a war that promised to end all wars. In its shocking ironies—the fatal clash of antique ideology and modern technology, the almost complete lack of cooperation between the European allies involved—the world war of 1914-18 had seemed just that, the worst the world was likely ever to see or suffer again. This pleasant fiction would endure another two decades until the Great War's second installment, again born in the heart of central Europe, could no longer be ignored by another America just as content to remain an island in a sea of other people's strife.

This soldier of that first great war has been laid to rest in a small, hilly burial ground near Silver Spring, Maryland, a few miles north of Washington DC. He spent his last weeks in the area and died quietly there in a sleep frequently interrupted by dreams. He was buried wearing chevrons acknowledging his service and the wounds he received during one of the war's most devastating clashes, the Meuse-Argonne offensive of September through November 1918. More American soldiers died in the forty-seven-day engagement than in any other conflict in U.S. history. He, smallest and most vulnerable of the troops, had lived.

Studding the freshly smoothed earth, which will soon sprout grass as the earth continues its turn toward summer, are several tiny, neat American flags that flit in the breeze. Where there is room for them, there are flowers. There will be flowers again next year, as well as a wreath left at Christmas time, still freshly green the following spring.

For a soldier of his age and one of his relative obscurity, he does not lack mourners, and not just those who, on hearing the sad news, made their way to the little cemetery to pay their respects—the officers and their wives, the members of his family, the friends who knew and loved him. His obituary and photograph were published in the *New York Times*, bumping celebrities and their glittering activities temporarily off their accustomed column space. Along with other lesser and greater newspapers across the country, the *Times* tells the story of his wartime adventures, his acts of bravery and bravado, the comfort he brought to so many in need of it.

As an officer who served with him, Brig. Gen. Lucius R. Holbrook, once reminded him at a military reunion: "We were together in France. I was your commander. You were at Soissons and in the Argonne. When your buddy was wounded you stuck to your duty and stayed with him till he was cared for."[1] Loyalty was this old soldier's singular trait and one that never left him, from wartime to peacetime. It was a loyalty that likely saved his own life, even as it saved the lives of others.

A few American poets were inspired to describe the veteran's military career and his life off the battlefield in verses lighthearted or rousing. H. I. Phillips wrote:

Sleeps he in some Valhalla,
Young and with new-found sight;
Waiting the drums, the bugles—
Getting his chance to fight![2]

New York journalist Minna Irving, herself nearly eighty, had been following the story of this soldier for some time. At the time of the Great War, in which the soldier had risked his life, Irving, a former staffer for the *New York Herald*, was best known for light love poems with titles such as "The Plaint of the Lover" or for stirring verses extolling patriotic deeds and ideals. But for this dead warrior two decades later, much older and wiser, Irving penned perhaps her most simply moving lines, a paean of mourning and a celebration of heroism. The brave soldier, Irving wrote, "faced shot and shell, and gas and smoke / In battle's crimson tide," and when he "mustered out," he did so "wearing still the glory of his scars."[3]

This soldier of the Great War was buried wearing marks of past glory but no uniform, because this soldier was a dog, a mutt of indefinable ancestry. The earth receiving him belongs to Aspin Hill Cemetery (later Aspin Hill Memorial Park), one of North America's oldest burial places for pets, those of everyday folks, as well as pets of the famous and some pets with fame of their own. The dogs of FBI director J. Edgar Hoover are buried here, as is Jiggs, the bulldog from the RKO *Our Gang* movies; in 1992 the park featured a memorial to the millions of lab animals who die in service to human science.

Our hero's name was Rags, a moniker inspired by his perpetually rumpled coat, a state of disarray with which he was most comfortable and which, on one memorable occasion, was subjected to a proper bath, an abomination Rags chose never to repeat. Starting out a homeless stray in Paris in the last months of World War I, Rags became mascot to the First Division of the American Expeditionary Forces a year after U.S. troops crossed the Atlantic to fight in their first European war. As General Holbrook correctly remembered, Rags was with the First Division at the crucial battle of Soissons, at Saint-Mihiel, and in the blood-and-mud bath of the Meuse-Argonne. In an incredibly brief period fraught with danger and distraction, Rags learned to run messages through gunfire, locate broken communications wire for the signal corps to repair, alert soldiers to incoming shells, and bring inspiration to men with little to hope for in the bitter last days of the war. Throughout his life, Rags had proved of what durable stuff one little dog is made.

As the years of peace between wars wound on, Rags became a necessary reminder to the human survivors of what it was that could hold men together, in heart and mind, when pushed past their limits by the thousand disasters of battle. Though other mascots were attached to certain units or even to certain soldiers, Rags belonged—if that word can be justly applied to a dog who lived very much according to his own will—to the entire First Division. But we may say that his guardianship circle was even wider than this. As Brig. Gen. Hugh A. Drum, who had known Rags in France in 1918, pointed out in the *New York Times* in 1926, if anybody actually "owned" Rags, it was "the great American public" itself. In the little flags left on his grave, this ownership was stated proudly, and poignantly.[4]

Human beings look down upon the world as at a map spread over a war-room table. Few of us not exploited ourselves have been brought up to look upon this map of the planet where we live and not consider it rightful that we should have dominion, as a well-known text contends, "over every creeping thing."

Had we studied this map of our world in the summer of 1917, our eyes would have fallen on a terrain scored by trenches and defense lines, each fresh wound or half-healed scar edged with opposing troops standing like tin soldiers set up by European rulers in high expectations of a conflict into which they had rushed so heedlessly. These figures would stand on the map from France in the north to Russia in the east and to Egypt in the south. Along with these men, representatives of a generation that wouldn't live long enough to know what they were supposed to be when they grew up, we would have seen the troops of another army: horses, mules, donkeys, oxen, camels, pigeons, dogs. All were summoned to take part in a conflict that even the most bloodthirsty warmonger would have to agree none had done anything to cause. Like fighting men, these animals offered the supreme sacrifice for the winning of a few acres of mud or sand, usually lost again that or the next day. Though many animals who assisted in past wars and occupation seemed eager to do their best by their human masters, it cannot be stated often enough that none of them was ever given a choice about whether or not they wanted to be there.

The words of French writer Gabriel Boissy, who as a Great War veteran first conceived the idea for an eternal flame over the grave of the Unknown Soldier in Paris, seem to speak to the fates of most animals who served in combat. "I dream of the dead that we left back there, half-buried," Boissy wrote. "Death is acceptable, certainly, but this oblivion, this abandonment, this anonymity?"[5] Though like these lost men and animals, Rags was also conscripted to the mayhem of human war, his story, though incomplete, is at least known. And though his star—what his first biographer called "the price of fame"—was briefly well in the ascendant, it fell as he and the soldiers who loved him aged, finally burning out. Almost a century since his battlefield exploits and the end of the war in which they occurred, Rags's known battlefield legacy and his wider life history are in need of reexamination. The first part of his life was filled with bursting bombs of war, but it did not end there. With the Armistice and Rags's smuggled journey to America, another life, just as full of drama and heartache, began.

Through Maj. Jack Rohan's 1930 book, *Rags: The Story of a Dog Who Went to War*, readers learned that there were two humans central to Rags's life. For several months between July 1918 till a month before Armistice Day, Rags was in the care of a First Division Signal Corps sergeant named Jimmy Donovan, who had taken him off the streets of Paris to the battlefields of the Western Front, teaching him techniques that helped save soldiers' lives, lying with him in the same trenches and shell holes and, in the end, on the same stretcher and in the same hospitals after both he and Rags were wounded at Hill 212 near the Forest of the Argonne. Then, from 1920 till his death sixteen years later, he came into the care of Maj. Raymond W. Hardenbergh, a former member of General Pershing's staff in France. Hardenbergh and his wife and daughters looked after Rags, making sure his legacy was recorded and remembered.

However, there was a third soldier in Rags's life, one who could claim an older and more crucial connection than anyone else besides Donovan. S.Sgt. George E. Hickman of the Sixteenth Infantry was present the day Rags was taken to First Division headquarters. Hickman fought with the Twenty-Sixth Division the day Rags carried his last and most famous message, and he was there to greet him ten years later for Rags's triumphant rediscovery in New York City as the division's hero-mascot, bearer of life-saving messages, good luck charm on four fluffy feet. Because Hickman's story, like most of the second installment of Rags's life, has never been told, it will be related in this book for the first time.[6]

Rags's life, set down in print almost ninety years ago by Major Rohan in a bold and well-intentioned effort mixing equal parts truth and sensationalism, has none of the glamour of Rin Tin Tin, the German shepherd rescued from a World War I foxhole to become an American movie star hero. Nor did Rags carry all the medals that adorned Sergeant Stubby, the brave and intelligent bull terrier of the 102nd Infantry, Twenty-Sixth Division; the most decorated canine mascot in history, Stubby also has the dubious distinction of still being on display, with his decorations, at the Smithsonian Institution.

Rags's legend is markedly different from Stubby's or from that of any other highly publicized military mascot. It was born against the shifting smoke and shifting memories of the battlefield, where events can be recalled with both photographic accuracy and the exaggeration of trauma but where heroism is rarely mistaken or forgotten. Rags's rediscovery and recognition as a war hero had a bright but brief blooming, fading in the run-up to another unimaginably brutal world war. But his story, perhaps more than that of any other military mascot, is still relevant today. It is the story of a dog rescued by a soldier who himself serves to rescue soldiers, an exchange of service that still takes place on military bases in South Asia and the Middle East today through the work of organizations like Nowzad, the British charity whose mandate is to save and organize adoptions for strays rescued by enlisted men and women.[7] It is also the story of Aspin Hill Memorial Park and the fierce battle that raged, first, over the placing of American flags on Rags's grave and, more than fifty years later, over all the graves as a community fought to save the cemetery from a commercial developer. And it is the story of a remarkable military family who, for over ninety years, has faithfully honored Rags's legend and his memory.

Rags's life speaks to the wider story of the courage and compassion humans and animals are capable of showing each other—and, in Rags's case, of compassion from animal toward animal as well—and of how that compassion lives on from battle to battle, from heart to heart, across oceans and across time. Rags's story is proof, as his biographer wrote, that "the war-worn soldiers of the First Division had room in their hearts for kindness to a homeless little dog." And as Maria Goodavage poignantly observes, "The irony is that soldier dogs make war a little more human."[8]

PART 1

Gutter Pup

O Lord of Humans,
make my master faithful to his
fellowmen as I am to him. . . .
Make him as good a man as I am a dog;
make him worthy of me, his dog.
—CAPT. WILL JUDY, friend of the Hardenbergh
family, "A Dog's Prayer for His Master"

1

The Hill of Mars

If numerous guesses add up to one true sum, the dog who would be known to history as First Division Rags—a scruffy, taffy-colored terrier of about twenty-five pounds, with floppy ears, fluffy arching tail, and perhaps more than a dollop of poodle in his blood—was born sometime in 1916.

By that year, Europe had been convulsed by war for twenty-four months. Few guessed at its beginnings that an archduke's assassination in a Balkan backwater would turn global bloodbath for the thrones on which the foundation of European society still stood and, worse, for international amity and the lives of an entire generation of lost young men.

By 1914 attempted and successful royal assassinations were hardly unheard of. Empress Elisabeth of Austria, beautiful and disturbed wife of long-time Emperor Franz Josef, had been stabbed to death in Switzerland in 1898; Queen Victoria had survived two assassination attempts, the second in 1882. Unlovable as bumptious Franz Ferdinand, heir presumptive to the Habsburg throne, had been, no crowned head in Europe but flinched on hearing that he and his wife had been gunned down with ease in Sarajevo on June 28, 1914, or that the assassin's job had been made easier thanks to the Serbian government's rumored links to the terrorist group to which the gunman belonged. Yet the archduke's demise on a Bosnian street corner might have remained second-page news, a solemn but not earth-shaking occasion for royal cousins to gather at the Habsburg crypt in Vienna, awaiting announcement of another heir to fill his place as the senescent Emperor Franz Josef lingered on his throne. But like a swift brushfire, the couple's deaths spread rapidly into the broader tragedy of Austria declaring war on Serbia and then to the greatest and most terrible one, of Russia,

3

Britain, and France joining Germany in lighting the powder keg of a war that blew most of civilization as people knew it to rubble.

Of one thing we can be sure. If Rags was really two years old, as claimed, when he fetched up in Montmartre (in the eighteenth arrondissement of Paris) in the summer of 1918, then, like children the same age, the terrier had never known a world not torn by war or a Paris that didn't cower by night.

Virtually from the start, the French capital had had to be on the qui vive for attack. It was the central prize of a German plan to encircle and knock out the French army, then move east to deal with Russia and break Germany's own encirclement by Britain and France. Zeppelins regularly came clanking over Paris, quiet bringers of disaster in payloads of bombs. The necessity of concealing potential targets meant that the city of light was often plunged into blackout—toward the war's end, Paris even laid out a miniature, fully illuminated doppelgänger sited safely outside the metropolis for zeppelins to drop their bombs on as they pleased.[1] Despite these wartime illusionist tricks, residents huddled in cellars, clutching hastily grabbed valuables and shushing terrified and confused children, and listened for the thud of impact and explosion, hoping it would not take place over their own heads. Throughout the war, this scenario was reenacted dozens of times in other cities, not just in Paris and France but in London and other parts of England, where war on British soil was not within anyone's living memory. And it was reenacted in Germany, too, where so many wars had happened and where more were to come, where other terrified and confused children came to know, as their own children would know, these same random explosions and this death that rained down from the black night air.

Far from the fraught world of the Great War, we have the luxury of sitting back and speculating at length about where Rags started out in life and how he survived in Paris. Was he born in a basket beside a stove or in the barn of one of the farms that still surrounded Montmartre in those days? According to his first biographer, Jack Rohan, Rags was terrified of automobiles but comfortable around and even friendly toward horses. Was this because he had spent his early life among farm horses outside the city, or because, as a street dog, he had gotten to know the draft horses that still clattered through pre–World War I Paris?

Though we can never know for sure, it's likely that Rags was in fact from high-lying Montmartre, the setting of his rescue, a district that had a history of being attractive to warriors of many kinds. The charming cobbled streets at the feet of quaint buildings had been the backdrop to or actual setting for warfare since the very first settlements around the hill on which Montmartre stood. Its name, despite Christianizing efforts to derive it from "hill of the martyrs," in fact started out as *mons martis*, or the hill of Mars, Roman god of war. It was the location of a temple raised to that violent deity and, allegedly, also a place of Druidic sacrifice, long before the promontory became associated with the martyred Saint Denis.[2]

Montmartre's height, made dramatic by its crowning structure, the Victorian wedding cake of the Basilique du Sacré-Coeur, often served a literally martial purpose, as when besieging armies sought to gain its slopes to pour firepower down on Paris below. A more lucrative result of these periodic influxes of soldiery were the many bars and nightclubs that sprang up in the district—the original "bistro," a word bestowed by early nineteenth-century Russian soldiers occupying Paris, is located in Montmartre. These establishments, along with prostitutes and their pimps, were drawn by cheap rents (more affordable the higher uphill you went), which is why nearly every fin de siècle artist from before and after World War I, as well as many writers, revolutionaries, working-class folk, and various creative eccentrics who straddled both worlds, also found a haven in Montmartre. These Bohemians, so-called because the French word for Gypsies seemed appropriate for people who lived unconventional lives, were there for a reason. By the time Rags first squirmed to life, Montmartre was changing. It was less sarcastic affront to proper Paris than gaudy self-caricature. No longer a powerful social statement, *la vie bohémienne* did rousing business among those it had once lampooned, and Montmartre was itself finally conquered by the crass commercialism and bourgeois values from which its residents had originally fled. Art was replaced by artifice; circuses arrived to exploit animals alongside bar shows exploiting women. The carnival atmosphere was only somewhat dampened by the advent of war.[3]

Rags had clearly adapted while young to the precarious realities of the streets. All his life, he demonstrated remarkable resourcefulness in finding venues offering not only good food but humans most apt to dispense it in a friendly manner. Prior to his rescue, his days and nights may have been spent searching for those friendly people. There would not have been as many as there were before he was born, because wartime Europe, thanks to overlapping blockades by Germany and Britain, was decidedly thin on food of any kind. Rags never knew his parents' prewar Paris of shops so overflowing with offal and leftover bread and cheese rind that shopkeepers could afford to toss them in the streets for mere dogs to devour. If there is much about his years as a stray that we cannot know and don't want to imagine, it is nonetheless easy to envision him waiting patiently for a handout outside Montmartre restaurants or bars, eating up whatever kitchen scraps they brought him and sometimes going hungry, as people were doing all around him.

Young Rags would have needed all the sustenance he could get. The winter of 1917, his first year of life, as described by an American diplomat in Paris, was one of the coldest on record, with bitter chill lasting into spring. And when not looking for food, Rags probably spent the rest of his time as other young strays did, learning to scurry between the feet of dance hall girls and ordinary pedestrians, avoiding horses' hooves and the heavy boots of policemen, surviving day by day.

Occasionally, of course, Rags would have stood stock still, watching and waiting, just as the people around him would do quite without warning. Even in wartime, Montmartre was noisy, its alleyways echoing with a cacophony of music, laughter, shouts, traffic. But Parisians knew, as from a sixth sense, when danger was overhead—like the shell dropped by a quiet dirigible one night in July 1917, landing not far from Montmartre, near the Gare du Nord, the all-important railway depot of Paris. "At about half-past eleven," wrote American diplomat John Gardner Coolidge, "just as I was getting to bed, we heard the sound of the siren, not very loud at first, but unmistakable, a doleful, wailing scream." Hurrying to the basement of their home, clutching jewels and silverware, the Coolidges didn't hear the impact of the bomb, but a keen-eared dog, scrounging for his dinner in nearby Montmartre, must have done so. And if he had already then perfected his method for dealing with such situations, Rags would probably have been found flat on his belly in an alleyway, much as he would do later on the battlefields of Picardy, until the danger had passed.[4]

Even in his lifetime, few would say that President Woodrow Wilson was not the personification of enigma.

Much of this was due to a greatly conflicted upbringing. Grandson of an abolition-minded newspaper editor from Ohio and Georgia-based son of a supporter of the Confederacy, Wilson spent a Southern child-hood among slaves in a setting that shaped his conservatism on race and on warfare. As a boy in Georgia, he remembered too well the massive upheaval of the Civil War, which to many north of the Mason-Dixon Line was rightful punishment for a rebel nation that had held slavery to be just, but to many south of it was a cruel invasion that had destroyed the fabric of a worthy and civilized society. On the one hand, Wilson generally held black people to belong to a lesser order of humanity. On the other hand, the only U.S. chief executive with a PhD, he embraced female equality, especially when the political benefits of doing so were pointed out to him; in fact, he trusted his wife, Edith, to such a degree that he relied on her to govern the nation for most of his second term as he lay in the White House incapacitated from a stroke. The door of Wilson's mind, if not wide open, was certainly well ajar.

Wilson put forward his Fourteen Points as an effort to secure peace for what he hoped would be all time, contributing to what would become the peace-keeping body of the United Nations. Before that, however, and for many for far too long, Wilson held off any kind of participation in the war one way or the other. After the liner *Lusitania* was torpedoed in 1915 by a German U-boat, killing 1,198 passengers and crew, includ-ing 128 Americans, Wilson forestalled entering the war for another two years, infuriating many Americans (though reassuring the business-men who made millions off trade in armaments and essentials with the enemy).[5] He contented himself, if no one else, by issuing toothless warnings over subsequent German breaches of international law. Yet his administration fanned the flames of latent American xenophobia to a degree only bested by explosively outraged former president Theodore Roosevelt, who since the war's start had declared another war on "the hyphenated [German-]Americans, the professional pacifists, the poltroon, the 'college sissy,' and the man with 'a mean soul.'"[6] Thanks to such rhetoric and to President Wilson's efforts to prepare the American consciousness for a war he could not avoid, all things German were condemned as suspicious. Even sauerkraut was renamed "liberty cabbage," not unlike the renamed "freedom fries" after 9/11.

When mobilization was finally ordered, on April 6, 1917, few American men were ready in even the most basic sense. Through the efforts of members of the Preparedness Movement, the praises of which were sung by men like Roosevelt, well-to-do volunteers had already been in training at camps across the nation. One of these camps was located at Plattsburgh, New York, the upstate military town that was to be the setting of Roosevelt's inflammatory speech on patriotism and manliness just as it would later be the setting for one of Rags's most memorable adventures. The Preparedness Movement has a familiar echo today. As in later American wars, demonization of the enemy was the primary means of whipping up support for conflict—in this case, the "Huns" were depicted as fiends with babies on the ends of their bayonets. The movement was also rooted in a single political party, in this case that of Republicans, who pressed a patriotism verging on the chauvinistic. It was very much along the lines of a crusade: weighty ballast like human rights and democratic process had to be cut loose so the overextended balloon of nationalism could fly higher and farther, preaching the gospel of holy war to all unbelievers.[7]

President Wilson had had this war-drum beating in his ears almost from the start; that he held off despite increasing taunts and threats says much, both positive and negative, about him as man and politician. Politically, he realized that the European war had already invaded America and was dividing a people who would need to be united if they were to truly be prepared to enter the fray (which, little did Americans realize, was itself a masterpiece of allied disunity). As a man, Wilson hated and feared conflict and such untidy situations as constituted the European war effort up to 1917, locked as it was in front-line standoffs that, chillingly, did not put a stop to the deaths of hundreds of thousands of men. Though he had an intellectual's distaste for everything to do with the military, of which he was commander in chief, Wilson likely also knew better than anyone that the United States was virtually incapable of waging the kind of battle needed to end the war. But this was barely a nick in the surface of what amounted to a lack not only of trained men but sufficient equipment for them to fight with, from rifles to cannon to ordnance. An added complication was the unseemly squabble, largely fueled by Britain but joined in by France, regarding how to manhandle U.S. general John J. Pershing, supreme commander of American forces, into allowing his troops to be subsumed under the Union Jack and the French tricolor, rather than fighting as Pershing insisted, as autonomous divisions under the American flag in association with Britain and France. (In 1917 British general Sir William Robertson went so far as to coldly suggest to Field Marshal Sir Douglas Haig that if only some American soldiers could get killed in skirmishes, Pershing might drop his insistence on American independence.)[8]

Three months after the U.S. declaration of war on Germany, on July 4, the worried General Pershing arrived in a Paris that was slightly drunken on unreasonable but understandable hopes for an American end to the endless European war. As Pershing and French president Raymond Poincaré watched from bunting-draped grandstands, a picked battalion of men of the American Expeditionary Forces (the Sixteenth Infantry) marched through the city to Les Invalides, burial site of Napoleon's restless remains. Pausing there by the bones of another dictator whose ambitions for empire had set Europe in flames, they marched on to the Cimitière de Picpus, burial place of Gilbert du Motier, marquis de Lafayette, American patriot by adoption (and noted dog lover), and his courageous wife, Adrienne. There, Pershing gave a salute at Lafayette's grave in thanks for an old but critical favor. At the head of a French army almost 150 years earlier, Lafayette had helped turn another hopeless battle to victory for the rebellious Americans against the British. Now, Pershing's act seemed to say, it was time to repay the debt. One of Pershing's staff, Col. Charles E. Stanton, put it best in just three words: "Nous voilà, Lafayette!" (Lafayette, we are here!). That was all the Americans could say at that early stage—they were "over there," as the popular American song refrain had it. Demanding though they

9

were at the best of times, many a French and British officer could be forgiven for saying, "Now what?" Pershing and his men had a steep hill to climb to prove that now that they were here, the terrible stalemate of the past three years could begin to crack, shift, and move like an icy river in spring thaw. Daunting, perhaps, for a less consummate—and compromising—soldier than John J. Pershing, but nonetheless worrisome. There was more to Black Jack Pershing than grit and buckram.[9]

A stiff-backed, disciplined, seemingly unemotional man whose outmoded tactics during the war would cost many American lives, General Pershing nevertheless had a soft center. Just two years before he was appointed to organize and direct the American army in the European war, he had lost his wife and most of his children in a freak house fire in the Presidio, the San Francisco military base where the Pershings lived. Only Pershing's six-year-old son, Warren, survived. As devastating as this tragedy was, however, it didn't harden Pershing's heart, nor did it limit his libido. Even as a married man, he was rumored to have a mistress in virtually every port of call and children left behind in the Philippines. Not long after arriving in Paris, Pershing took up with a French-Romanian artist named Micheline Resco. Though small of stature, Resco was large of heart, with a smile that could light up a city block. Whatever truth there was to the rumors of the kind of women who typically attracted Pershing, Resco was no fly-by-night, either as a person or as an artist. She painted one of the most penetrating portraits of Pershing, visual evidence of an enduring love and deep understanding of an otherwise inscrutable personality. In 1946, two years before he died, the sick and elderly Pershing made an honest man of himself and married Resco while he was a patient at Walter Reed Hospital.[10]

Pershing would prove he had a tender heart for his men also, especially for those who had given the fullest measure of a soldier's devotion. For a 1919 Memorial Day service at Romagne Cemetery, established several months earlier on green slopes between the river Meuse and the Argonne Forest, Pershing labored over his address. Deliberate in all things and hating to speak in public, Pershing had to make his speech right, not just for the living attending the service in the largest American cemetery in Europe but for the dead. Indeed, especially for them. One morning in the turreted splendor of the Château du Val des

Écoliers, his wartime HQ near Chaumont, Pershing called on his aide, Col. John G. Quekmeyer, as he had something to read to him. Colonel Quekmeyer found Pershing in a bathrobe with sheets of paper on his lap, the pages furrowed with crossed-out passages, the margins crawling with asides, blurred by multiple erasures. Placing his spectacles on his nose and lifting the pages to the light, Pershing read the entire address, which ended with these words: "It is not for us to proclaim what they did. Their silence speaks more eloquently than words. It is up to us to uphold that for which they died. . . . Dear comrades, farewell." "As he reached the last lines," wrote Marquis James, the Pulitzer Prize–winning author and journalist for the *American Legion Weekly*, "Pershing's voice grew husky and then ceased. . . . 'Quekmeyer,' said Pershing, 'I don't know whether I can say it or not.'"[11]

Though love for women and for one's troops don't necessarily go hand in hand with compassion for animals, in Pershing's case they did. In 1908 Pershing was asked to intercede for a hero of the Fifth Field Artillery, a handsome, solid, and faithful horse named Putnam who had served not just at Fort Hamilton in New York City but also in Cuba, the Philippines, and most famously Beijing during the Boxer Uprising. The first day American troops arrived outside the Imperial City, Putnam alone pulled up a steep hill a massive field gun that had broken away from the other horses that had been assisting him in the job; this was the gun used to fire the first shot at the city. After the uprising, Putnam, renamed Peking, went back to his duties in the Philippines, where because of his age he was in danger of being "sold to the Manila cart peddlers," as Col. Edward T. Brown warned. So Colonel Brown appealed to General Pershing, who immediately agreed, as did the secretary of war, that Peking deserved a comfortable retirement. Not many military powerhouses would have found the time to intercede for an elderly horse, but it is not surprising that Pershing did so. Nor is it surprising that he also loved dogs—as a schoolteacher, he had once whipped one of his students not for refusing to do his schoolwork but for kicking a dog that had found its way into the classroom. In 1921 Pershing would take obvious pleasure in awarding a gold medal to Sergeant Stubby, mascot of the 102nd Infantry, Twenty-Sixth Division. Stubby was famed for, among other things, saving an entire unit from a gas attack. But he also helped American soldiers by giving them what to most American men of the time was the familiar, loving presence of a dog, something of normal life to focus on and cherish in the unfamiliar hell of war. Photos taken the day Stubby was medaled give evidence of Pershing's gentle touch, and his tender look conveys both his respect and his affection for one little dog who could save lives while raising morale—achievements as important on a battlefield as tactics or firepower, whether they are accomplished by a dog, a mule, a cat, or a pigeon.[12]

That Independence Day of 1917 in Paris, General Pershing wrote in his memoirs that he, much like a curious dog, moved not within the marching soldiers but alongside them, driving from street to street in an effort to see the men and the reaction to them from as many possible angles as he could. Amid all the fluttering American and French flags and motorcades ferrying dignitaries from historic site to historic site and the cheering crowds pelting the green and grinning young Americans with flowers, did Rags find his way down the hill from Montmartre? As General Pershing zigzagged along the march route, was he followed by a pair of bright brown eyes?[13]

2

A Dog's Life

Efforts to reconstruct the circumstances of Rags's whereabouts before he entered the lives of two American soldiers are complicated by radically different versions of how and when his rescue occurred.

One of the soldiers died without leaving a written account. The surviving soldier was never quoted verbatim by journalists and left no known notes about exactly how the rescue happened. And so the story morphed in the retelling, through the memory of surviving doughboys, stretched to distortion by the passage of time and the page-turning exaggerations introduced by newsmen over the ensuing decades. To this latter group belongs Rags's first biographer, Maj. John Joseph "Jack" Rohan, an adroit and perceptive newspaperman.

Born in Tennessee in October 1884, Rohan spent most of his professional career as an editor and journalist in the Midwest and in New York State.[1] When he registered for the draft in September 1918, he was thirty-four years old and living in Morris, Illinois, working as managing editor of the *Morris Herald*. Rohan seems to have been immediately promoted to the rank of major, which may be explained by the fact that a lack of officers toward the end of the war made it necessary to promote rapidly in the American forces. Intelligent and street-smart, Rohan was appointed to a branch dealing with communications, where his reporter's talents could be put to best use (as they were again during World War II). He may have served in that capacity right up to and beyond November 11, 1918, until returning to his former profession. After World War II, Rohan, then author of a biography of Samuel Colt, the Connecticut firearms inventor, would claim a colorful military career. According to the dust jacket blurb, "Lieutenant Colonel [*sic*] Jack Rohan" was "a professional newspaperman and an amateur soldier," though according to his history, it is a wonder he had time to keep to a journalist's deadlines. The blurb claims Rohan "fought in revolutions in Honduras, Nicaragua and Mexico, and saw service in both world wars, during the more recent as a lieutenant colonel on the General Staff in Washington." How Rohan was involved in the three revolutions is not stated. However, his work in Washington is well attested.[2]

Given his flair for drama (of which Rags's human family in America was well aware), it is no surprise that for the opening scene in his biography of Rags, Rohan chose a dark-and-stormy approach—despite the fact that this probably was not the way it happened at all.[3]

According to Rohan, late on the night of July 14, 1918, in the winding streets of Montmartre, with air-raid alarms hanging in the air along with the threat of German shells, a private (later sergeant) of the First Division Signal Corps named Donovan who was attached to the Seventh Field Artillery exited a Montmartre bar and realized he was lost.

Donovan was among a group of American soldiers hand-picked from his company to march on parade in Paris to celebrate Bastille Day. "Donovan's captain was lenient in such little matters as unauthorized absence for a few hours of sight-seeing," wrote Rohan. However, it was doubtful his leniency would have stretched far enough to cover skipping the strict curfew. "To be missing when the outfit moved was desertion," Rohan tells us. Donovan stepped carefully through the alleyways, searching the sky "in hope of finding a star by which to orient himself," unable to ask directions because, like most doughboys, he spoke no French. "He had picked a few cautious steps," wrote Rohan, "when his foot bumped something soft and yielding," which Donovan took to be a pile of rags. However, this pile of rags made sounds—it whimpered at the unintended kick, then stood up and barked. It was a dog. Donovan lit a match to see what kind of dog and promptly was ordered to douse the light by American military police, who had stolen up unawares. Rohan tells us that Donovan's reflex was to pick the dog up and hold it in his arms, a fragile kind of protecting barrier between himself and the gruff MPS. Unamused, the MPS ordered Donovan to follow them. During his march to the American military police post in Montmartre, Donovan explained that he was not AWOL and that the dog was in fact the company mascot; Donovan was late because he had been out and about looking for the dog. Asked for the dog's name,

Donovan, according to Rohan, responded readily: "Rags, sir." Rags jumped down to the ground and snuggled against Donovan's booted feet, apparently solidifying his alibi.[4]

Let's hold the scene there for a moment while we, like the (possibly fictitious) MPs, check out the bona fides of this soldier. Who was the resourceful, dog-loving Donovan? In fact, much about him is a complete mystery. Neither in *Rags* nor in newspaper articles predating the book is he even assigned a first name. Only with Rags's 1936 *New York Times* obituary do we stumble over his name, much as Donovan was said to have tripped in the dark over Rags while at the same time stumbling over the other soldier who was with him, though not accounted as such by Rohan. "At his headquarters on Governors Island," reads the text, "Sergeant George Hickman of the Sixteenth Infantry, recalled the least bit vaguely that day almost nineteen years ago when he and Private Jimmy Donovan emerged from a Montmartre café after a post-parade celebration." Rohan tells us precious little else than this. From him, we learn that Donovan was born in the Midwest and that though in the Great War he served in the United States Army Signal Corps, he had served years earlier under Col. (later Brig. Gen.) Halstead Dorey in the Philippines, in what capacity Rohan does not describe. Rohan tells us that Donovan was promoted from private to sergeant in 1918, around the time Rags came into his life. Aside from these details and the inference that Donovan was brave under attack and was clearly a superb dog trainer, we know nothing else about him. That is likely to remain the case. The destruction of the majority of World War I service records in a fire at the National Personnel Records Center in 1973 may forever close the door on this subject. It doesn't help that Rohan's reasonably fact-based narrative in *Rags* is spliced with colorful and probably invented vignettes illustrative of life in the American trenches and mess tents of France. "Five [*sic*] years ago," runs the 1936 obituary, "a biography of Rags had it that Donovan alone found the animal, that it happened late one night, that the soldier was AWOL, and that an MP brought both back to army jurisdiction"—strongly implying that none of these events had happened as Rohan described them.[5] Several years before Rohan's book was published, the *New York Times* reported in two separate articles from 1925 that Rags actually *followed* Donovan of his own accord from a café in broad daylight—a far cry from Rohan's image of the dog being fetched cowering and hungry off a dark and rainy street, aligning with what Hickman remembered, and possibly informed by his uncredited recollection.[6]

Why wasn't Hickman consulted? Given Rohan's superior military rank and the fact that most of the identifiable men he seems to have talked to for his book were senior officers, including Maj. Raymond W. Hardenbergh, Rags's guardian at the time, perhaps Rohan overlooked Hickman or did not seek him out. Or maybe the omission was by choice. Perhaps Hickman believed that such a different version of long-accepted events, cemented in place by Rohan's best-selling book, might confuse or compromise Rags's history and the honors that he deserved. Protectiveness toward Rags would certainly be a signal characteristic of Hickman's relationship with him, just as it had been with Donovan.

By comparison with Donovan (and thanks to a family that saved every letter he wrote and picture he took), we know a great deal about Hickman both as a soldier and as a civilian. Born in Nicholas, West Virginia, in 1890, Hickman had joined the armed forces as early as 1915. He fought in the battle of Agua Prieta in Mexico and then served with the First Division in France from 1917 till Armistice. With the First Division, he took part in all the major American engagements, including Cantigny in May 1918. In that battle, Hickman sustained no fewer than seven gunshot wounds, landing him in the hospital. But according to a letter Hickman wrote his sister on July 28, 1918, he was discharged from his hospital on July 12, and as his last known whereabouts prior to this date place him en route to Vichy from a French *hôpital complémentaire* (an administrative category, along with *hôpitals auxiliaires* and *hôpitals bénévolés*) in Toulouse in June 1918, he had plenty of time, and a healthy if painful body, to have joined his comrades in arms in Paris for the Bastille Day celebrations a month later.[7]

To Hickman's grandchildren, it is no surprise that he played a role in the life story of one of history's most famous military mascots. All his life, Hickman loved dogs. While in training camp before shipping over to France, Hickman was photographed playing with a Jack Russell terrier, a dog that evidently meant a great deal to him, because he kept photos taken of him with it till the end of his life. And when he was wounded at Cantigny, right beside him was another dog, a bull-dog mascot he called Dick. "I bought him from Madam Stouvanot (a French Lady) July 1917," Hickman explained to his sister a year later, "and he is a real mascot. . . . [He] has been with us all the time on the front and he was with me when I got wounded also, one of my friends took him to the Doctor and had him operated on and when I came back he was limping around with a hole through his front leg but he is well."[8] It is tempting to speculate whether the friend who helped was Jimmy Donovan.

The keeping of military mascots has an even longer history than the word "mascot" itself, a Latin-derived term referring to magic and the people or objects conferring it. The magic of having an animal companion in the midst of battle has always held a mystique verging on religious fervor. Regulations were long ago set in place curtailing the keeping of any animals other than those used for battle purposes, but throughout history these rules have been more honored in the breach than in the observance—even today, on bases from Afghanistan to Europe and Asia, soldiers will risk much to help and protect a friendly stray dog or cat.[9]

A mascot (and not all were dogs—there were cats, coyotes, bears, goats, and many other kinds of animals) could be a gift to a regiment or brought along by one of the men. Some dogs, like the Irish terrier Prince, joined a soldier or an entire unit of their own volition. As Ernest Harold Baynes wrote in *Animal Heroes of the Great War*, when Private Brown of the First North Staffordshires left for France with his regiment in August, shortly after the outbreak of war, he left behind a very upset Prince to be looked after by his wife. A month later, Mrs. Brown could not find Prince and decided he had simply run away. A few weeks after, however, her husband sent her a letter, announcing that Prince was with *him*. As Private Brown wrote, "It is a very strange thing that I should have got him. A man brought him to me from the front trenches. I could not believe my eyes until I got off my horse and he made a great fuss over me. I believe he came over with some other troops." Another dog, an English setter, is known to have followed his guardian and shared with him the first battle of the Marne. He was with his soldier when the latter was buried by an exploding mortar shell, and the dog was able to dig him out. The dog, also injured, limped behind the ambulance to the hospital. When he followed the stretcher-bearers in, someone talked of putting him outside. "But when the head nurse heard the story," Baynes wrote, "she exclaimed, 'He has as good a right here as any of us have.'"[10]

Though Sergeant Stubby was the most famous of the mascot dogs deliberately smuggled overseas on troop ships, another, less well known but with just as much charisma, was Don, half-collie, half-shepherd. Don was donated by his patriotic guardian to the Twenty-Third Regiment of the New York National Guard at Yorktown, which then was reconstituted as Company B, 106th Infantry of New York, in May 1917. When it came time for the regiment to sail for Europe, "the rules of embarkation of the Army which forbade the taking of animals overseas meant nothing to Don," runs a post-Armistice article. "He had enlisted for the war and intended to see it through." How he was finally smuggled aboard ship was, unsurprisingly (as later with Rags), "a carefully guarded military secret." According to the regiment's record, Don served "through every battle, engagement and minor action in which [the regiment] took part" and "has a service record of which any American soldier might be proud." Don was wounded at Vierstraat Ridge in Belgium on September 2, 1918, "by a machine gun bullet in the left foreleg" and injured on the Hindenburg Line later that month by shrapnel in the right foreleg. Capt. Robert H. Trask recorded in Don's service record under "Remarks" that he was "fearless, true and always faithful to his comrades." Don was entitled to two wound stripes and a stripe for his six months of service. "Being a good mascot, he may wear the Division insignia," the report says. "Request is made that Don be given a position in the line when the Regiment parades in New York or Brooklyn."[11]

Mascots like Stubby were able to easily cross the line, going from comforting presence in the trenches to active participants in battle alongside their soldiers. "They have done sentry duty in the trenches and, with their masters, patrol duty out on No Man's Land," wrote Ernest Harold Baynes and his coauthor, Louis Agassiz Fuentes, in *The Book of Dogs*. These versatile dogs carried critical dispatches over and under the tangled shrubbery of barbed wire and through rain-flooded shell craters in which men and horses drowned. These dogs also dodged the shellfire which created those craters, as when they were given the supremely critical task of safely delivering across their backs the light-weight baskets holding the dispatch pigeons on whose homing instincts the lives of entire regiments depended. These dogs also served a no less vital purpose when some of them, "each with a big can of hot soup strapped to either side, [were] sent through the front-line trenches to carry this cheering fare for the fighting men," Baynes and Fuentes wrote. These dogs refused to stay behind. They had to be where their soldiers were; they had to share whatever their soldiers experienced, even when that sharing was costly or fatal.[12]

At this point, then, let us turn back to Rags where Rohan left him, sitting there on a cobbled Parisian street in the path of pedestrians whose feet did not always take care to avoid him.

It's clear enough that Hickman and Donovan were fully primed for their meeting that July afternoon with a scruffy stray begging outside their café. We can understand what drew them to him. What was it that would draw a street dog to two soldiers? Rags was used to a hard life, a life of grabbing what he could when he could, a life in which there was as much famine as feast, as many kicks as caresses. To most Parisians, strays were in the way; they were carriers of disease; they were dirty and smelly thieves, overturning ripe trashcans, fighting over bones and offal, mating and creating more strays just like them, all better off dead.

Rags's experience of people pivoted on negotiating with this attitude on an hourly basis, his continued survival in the balance at all times. He must have been initially wary of human interference in his accustomed routine, which was not one of choice but of a survival that didn't allow him time to pause and ponder anything different. Yet when the two soldiers emerged from the café, bent down to ruffle his ears and to give him a scrap of pastry, talking to him as kind men do when they meet a dog, then walked away, Rags was faced with a choice. Perhaps he had sometimes trailed others who had given him something to eat or a scruff on the head and been shooed away or lost his would-be rescuer in the crowds along the thoroughfare. This time, though, Rags persisted. Did he want to see where he could get more of that scrap of pastry? Or was it that nobody, until these two men appeared from the café, had ever shown him this kindness before? Possibly it was a combination of all of the above, and maybe of something else: Rags seems to have sensed that though he was in need, *he* was needed, too.

Whether it happened as Rohan wrote or as Hickman suggested, the rest falls neatly into place.

Noticing that the dog was still at their heels, Hickman and Donovan patted his head again and told him to go home—not knowing that he had no home. Persuasion unavailing, and one of the men being clearly more smitten with the terrier than the other (Hickman had his own mascot back at his unit), Rags peeled off with Donovan, trotting into the lens of history. And when rescuer and dog had to face the curfew patrol, Rags at once showed how grateful he was, if Rohan's account is to be believed. Rohan says that in the truck to which the AWOL Donovan was marched by MPs, to face the music at the commandant's headquarters, Rags so thoroughly charmed the police sergeant escorting Donovan that by the time they arrived, he had successfully aided and abetted his soldier in the fiction of searching for the lost mascot (or taken the sergeant's mind off Donovan's alleged crime). Donovan was off the hook as deserter, and French-speaking Rags was receiving his first English lessons (courtesy of the bilingual mess sergeant), along with his baptismal rookie ration with the First Division of the American Expeditionary Forces.

What happened in Montmartre on Bastille Day 1918 was an ironic rescue for a dog who had probably experienced no battles other than between himself and other dogs over the spoils of café refuse.

The real thing, at least in human terms, was soon coming. In just another four days, the First Division would join forces with the French to attack Soissons, sixty-five miles northeast of Paris, breaking a stalemate with the German army that had lasted some thirty-six months. Rags would show, even in what was to him the utterly alien battlefield landscape of trees lashed to bare sticks by bullets, of mud and filth stretching for miles toward every horizon, and of more sudden, more deadly bursts of bombs than he would ever have experienced in a Paris air raid, that a street mutt could learn the art of war every bit as easily as he picked up slang like "chow." In the jaunty martial parlance of the day, Rags was already learning to "do his bit."[13]

3

War Dog

Be comforted, little dog, Thou too in the Resurrection shalt have
a tail of gold.

—MARTIN LUTHER

At the outbreak of hostilities, the German army's military dog program
had the jump on Britain, with several thousand carefully trained canines
to the United Kingdom's single one. But by 1917, Col. Edwin Richardson
had been given permission to establish a training center for war dogs
at Shoeburyness in Sussex, and the imbalance was soon redressed.[1]

As in all times of war, patriotism sometimes trumped common sense.
Because it was seen as one's duty to do as much for the cause as possible,
many English families found a way to participate by donating animals
they owned, whether horses or dogs—and in dog- and horse-loving
Britain, these were very significant donations indeed. All familiar with
Michael Morpurgo's novel *War Horse* have a sense of how badly things
could go for horses sent away from the green fields of England. Many
do not know just how badly things could also go for the donated dogs.

While one horse is useful in much the same way as another (there
being major variations on the shape and size available), donated dogs
presented opportunities, challenges, and the potential for tragedy. The
dog breeds deemed most useful for message delivery were Airedale
terriers, but other breeds were considered capable of serving in different
capacities. Unfortunately, those judged unsuitable by temperament,
breed, or size for war work were not always returned to their guardians;
many were summarily put down, without their guardians knowing
their fates then or ever.

Jilly Cooper, author of *Animals in War*, tells of an especially heartbreaking account. According to Cooper, one English owner gave to the

War Department a King Charles spaniel, believing it could be of service in battle. As we will see, size and breed were certainly no barriers to battlefield success. The unfortunate spaniel, however, cowering and immobilized by fear, was shot before ever reaching France.[2]

For many acceptable dogs who did make it through training and on to the front, there was a sad end to a happy beginning. One of these was Dick, a black retriever. According to Colonel Richardson, Dick's was "a wonderful record, worthy of the V.C." Early in the war, Dick carried a message in the Villers-Bretonneux sector (Somme department), during which he received wounds to his back and shoulder. "The dog completed his run in good spirit," recalled Colonel Richardson, "and was ultimately sent back to the section kennel for treatment from the veterinary officer." But the vet was possibly distracted that day; finding no reason to operate, he stitched up Dick's wounds. Dick performed several more message runs before he began manifesting symptoms of pain. He deteriorated to the point where the vet had no recourse but to euthanize him. "At the post-mortem examination," wrote Colonel Richardson, "it was discovered that a rifle bullet was resting between the shoulder and body, while near the small of the back a piece of shrapnel was found lodged close to the spine." Despite the pain he was in, Dick had "carried out his duties cheerfully and most faithfully."[3]

No matter the dangerous conditions, overwork, and starvation, there were triumphs of good luck and extraordinary heroism for animals in combat. A lurcher and deerhound cross named Major—"not much to look at"—was at first not taken seriously as messenger material. Yet when challenged to prove himself, he did so again and again. He "beat the [human] runners every time," wrote Colonel Richardson, "and never made one mistake." On just one of Major's message runs, he passed too close to an enemy artillery battery. The guns opened up. "I could see that Major was actually dodging the shells," stated a witness. "He took a wide sweep from where the first shell fell, and kept working out farther," a scene thrilling and harrowing to envision. Major's most shining moment was when he succeeded in carrying through a desperate request for reinforcements. For that run, "Major did 17 kilometers in one hour," wrote an admiring Colonel Richardson.[4]

A famous photograph from the war shows a large, sleek hound from the German side, its message collar visible, as it vaults a trench twice its length, every sinew pulled forward like an arrow toward its target. However, big dogs were by no means the only ones capable of running messages through no-man's-land, where size could be a liability. One example was "Little Jim," a black terrier-Pomeranian cross. Little Jim ran so fast, breaking time records of all the other dispatch dogs in his sector, that few soldiers had ever really seen him in action, though many had benefited from his bravery. Colonel Richardson was told by an Australian officer of his first impressive glimpse of another seemingly ineligible dispatch dog. The dog was especially interesting to the officer because it was neither a lurcher nor a retriever but a Welsh terrier, the size of Rags, perhaps (like Little Jim) a household pet given to the military. "The ground it was going over was in a terrible condition," the officer described to Colonel Richardson, "and was absolutely waterlogged. The little creature was running along hopping, jumping, plunging, and with the most obvious concentration of purpose. [The officer] could not imagine what it was doing until it came near, and he saw the message carrier on its neck. As the dog sped past him he noticed the earnest expression on its face."[5]

These official messenger dogs on either side of the conflict had had to pass grueling tests of desensitization to explosions, smoke billows, and the rest of the arsenal they were likely to be exposed to. To these dogs was applied everything described in vivid detail by an American officer, Lt. Col. Ashby Williams, and endured by every man in the trenches: "One can only feel, one cannot describe, the horror that fills the heart and mind. . . . [Y]ou hear the explosion like the single bark of a great dog in the distance, and you hear the deadly missile singing as it comes towards you, faintly at first, then distinctly, then louder and louder until it seems so loud that everything else has died, and then the earth shakes and the eardrums ring, and dirt and iron reverberate through the woods and fall about you."[6] In such an atmosphere of aural and visual violence, it could never be clear whether dogs like the terrier glimpsed by the Australian officer were running with conscious effort to bring their message back to an artillery post or whether they were simply running for their lives to escape the same noisy hell of shellfire that soldiers like Lieutenant Colonel Williams endured and that Major had had to outfox and outrun.

Men fight wars for a variety of reasons, but most understand why they are fighting, or at least have had a choice about whether or not to do so. Animals serve at the mercy of humans who control them, with no opt-out clause in the contract. It is troubling to think of a twenty-pound street dog like Rags being exposed to the smoke, noise, and fire of war, which could reduce even experienced men to hysteria. Yet the mystery of it all is just how easily Rags seemed to adjust. Life on the streets of Paris would have exposed him to the rattle and clank of horse-drawn conveyances and wagons and the backfiring of the automobiles gradually populating the cobbled streets. He had lived through more than one zeppelin bomb raid over Paris. But the blast of explosives at close range was surely something new. A dog's hearing is vastly more sensitive than a man's, capable of detecting sound at higher frequencies than humans are able to do, and in addition aiding dogs in determining the depth, height, and direction of a given sound, such as the approach of a shell. Soldiers were often left with shell shock after two or three days of exposure; occasionally, some even died from the trauma.

Only in his elder years, when the comparatively tiny explosions of flash photography would startle him into confusion, did Rags appear to have lost the iron nerves imputed to him during the violent battles he took part in through the last three months of the war. But throughout his service in the Great War, never far from the cacophony of the Seventh Field Artillery, Rags proved able to not only stand it but carry out his duties as directed.

That Rags seemed able to reason out the dangers around him, rather than panicking, and know what to do when confronted by them is made clear by one of Rohan's anecdotes. Like Sergeant Stubby, well known for alerting soldiers to dangers they could not hear, one of Rags's first efforts as mascot of the First Division occurred en route to Soissons. He suddenly fell flat, "as close to the ground as his little body could get," wrote Rohan. As with Stubby, the first time it happened, the men thought this belly flop amusing. When they finally heard the incoming shell as it whined overhead, they, too, dropped to the ground, and—as Rags clearly expected—the shell exploded close by. From this time on, wrote Rohan, Donovan and all the men who knew Rags paid close attention to his reactions, noting that before he ducked to the ground he usually gave a "growling little bark."[7] (In fact, dogs did not corner the market on these uncanny abilities. Earlier in the war, British soldier Albert Martin of the 122nd Signal Coy, Forty-First Division, Royal Engineers, remarked on a kitten who "can appreciate the difference in direction and also understand that danger comes from one direction only.")[8]

Rags seemed to understand that the noise and danger were going to get worse before they got better, and he was correct. As the artillery unit drew closer to Soissons, the explosions only grew louder, the tremors stronger. "This melee went on from July 15–16, with July 17 being the worst of all," states the Seventh Field Artillery history. "All day long, the road from Compiègne Forest through the narrow streets of Mortefontaine was packed tight with artillery of all calibres." That night, a rainstorm completed the men's misery. For hours, lightning flashed as groups of men soaked to the skin struggled with overworked horses and stalled engines to shift ordnance and supplies through a slippery mire. "H-hour"—the set time for commencement of combat—came, and with it the storms of the night dissolved into a dawn "sweet and peaceful, giving evidence of a beautiful summer day over the wheat fields," writes the Seventh Field Artillery historian. In such a setting, familiar to so many of the men from their rural American boyhoods, there was "little evidence of the death struggle to come."[9] But that struggle emerged soon enough with daylight, though nothing the sun offered could compete with the artificial brilliance of American barrage shelling. "I will never forget the sight when our artillery opened up," wrote Private William Francis of the Second Division. "It was worse than any electrical storm I have ever seen." Maj. Raymond B. Austin, an officer with the field artillery who, before being killed in action that October, left many written impressions of what it was like fighting this war, was similarly impressed by the barrage. "It made the ground tremble," he wrote, "and every hill and valley was just a mass of flashes in the dim light of early morning."[10]

Soon after arriving at his artillery post, Donovan began having doubts that he should have brought Rags this far into the battle zone, an indication that his adoption of the dog, like the adoption of many military mascots, had been undertaken without due consideration of the consequences of what might happen to the animal in the event of actual warfare. For a doughboy who had already flirted with prosecution for appearing to desert his unit in Paris, Donovan was obviously ready to risk his neck again. With jump-off near, Donovan had little time to rush Rags back to division headquarters. Explaining to a sergeant major what was going on, Donovan then hurried back to Coeuvres-et-Valsery, where the Seventh Artillery was waiting for its orders and for him.

Only after arriving did Donovan find his good deed undone, because there, sitting beside him, a panting but happy escapee, was Rags.

If, as we have seen, a central tragedy of the use of animals in combat situations is that none of them is given a choice as to whether they want to be there, Rags was a different animal altogether. His choice seems to have been to be with Donovan wherever he was, regardless of the dangers or even of what Donovan would have preferred—a signal trait of most dogs, but especially poignant in a rescued stray.[11]

4

A Match Made in Hell

The typical Hollywood film makes it all too easy to stereotype, and misrepresent, warfare.

From safe seats in dark cinemas redolent of popcorn and bubblegum, we observe a series of scenes filled with closely packed explosions, diving planes, hand-to-hand combat, and soldiers advancing through bullet-shattered forests, during which men become superhuman beings who never sleep, video game heroes who don't really die.

Superficially, war *is* all that sound and fury. And war is also the quiet forlornness of death. War is the mute corpses of humans and animals, captured in the photographic accuracy of their final agonies. It is bullet-riddled and abandoned farmhouses and barns and churches. It is silent refugees carrying all they possess on their backs, trudging weary miles along muddy tracks from villages that have ceased to exist or that, somehow worse, still lift bomb-shattered bits of wall like gravestones lurching across a country cemetery. War is barren barbed wire and wasted wheat churned to mire, and it is living animals, laboring in the war machine or preserving the comparative semblance of normalcy in cratered fields, voicelessly enduring whatever comes.

Nor is war without peace, or at least brief spates of it carved out of the dense, deafening noise. Relieved units taken out of battle for rest cooled their heels in some spot not far enough away from the battlefield to escape the explosions that are some other unit's fight.

These pauses in the relentless action often occurred in settings surreal in their apparent normalcy, as remarked on by many soldiers. Second Lt. Alexander Gillespie of the Second Argyll and Sutherland Highlanders wrote in his diary of watching the moon rise and hearing a nightingale sing, "all the more sweetly and clearly in the quiet intervals between the bursts of firing." Experiencing a similar short lull, Second

Lt. Wilfred Ewart of the First Scots Guards found the sensation more sobering. "It is from this," he wrote in 1916, "this pageant of peace and plenty and beauty, that one goes into the bloody nightmare of battlefields." Looking up at the stars, Lieutenant Ewart wondered what they might say to the soldier who, earthbound still, asked himself, Is this my last chance to look at them?[1]

Jimmy Donovan also had these interludes of warlessness within war. During the Soissons offensive, when he wasn't servicing damaged communications wire, Donovan used his valuable rest time to get to know Rags better and to find out what job the little dog wanted to perform in this war, since he refused to be mustered out of it. Donovan was aware by now that garden-variety tricks were of no interest to Rags. He was not in the trenches to entertain, like the stray kittens some troops took in, the playing and bravado of which during heavy fighting were both distraction and inspiration. This was made clear when some of the artillerymen had attempted to teach Rags to fetch a ball or to jump through their hooped arms. He turned his back to them, as if insulted, like a busy farm or herding dog with far too many responsibilities to put up with such human childishness. "Every dog is extremely susceptible to ridicule," wrote R. H. Smythe. "It enjoys laughter, providing one is laughing with it, but becomes extremely embarrassed and unhappy if it even suspects that it is being made fun of."[2]

Concluding that Rags might best enjoy learning to do things that produced results (and if that was something that helped Donovan in his own work, all the better), the sergeant decided to teach Rags how to carry messages. In a war in which highly trained dispatch dogs were standard for the British, French, and German armies, Donovan's plans set the bar very high for both himself and his dog.

How he achieved this—and why he was allowed leave to do so, since, as we know, having a mascot at all was against army regulations—with so little time for needed practice, rehearsal, and trial runs, and that he did it so well, is astonishing, considering what he had to work with.[3] Colonel Richardson had selected such dogs very carefully. If a dog was to ever be in a position to successfully carry a message on which lives and the outcomes of battles might depend, it had to be disciplined, fearless under fire. Rags was a stray fresh off the streets of Paris, from the nightclub district no less—not even a dog with what Colonel Richardson would consider useful peacetime working experience. And looking at his strong attachment to Donovan, it was doubtful Rags could ever fulfill Colonel Richardson's most basic requirement. "The dog has to work entirely on its own initiative and be miles away from its keeper," explained Colonel Richardson. "It has to know what to do, and to think out how it is going to do it. It is easy to understand, therefore, that the messenger dog has to be trained in such a way that it takes the keenest delight and pride in its work."[4]

"The training of a messenger dog requires a decidedly special gift in the instructor," asserted Richardson. "Without a long, intimate, and practical working experience among dogs on a large scale, no one need attempt to train messenger dogs in war-time. . . . [T]he most important point in the whole messenger service is this question of the keepers. It is more important than that of the dog."[5] In the colonel's highly successful training scheme, dogs were subjected to a program lasting weeks if not months, beginning with selecting the appropriate breed, then pairing each dog with the appropriate handler, and finally testing the dogs thus chosen by confronting them with water hazards, smoke and shell barrages, and obstacle courses of barbed wire and broken terrain. Richardson does not actually describe how his dogs were trained to take a message from one place to another (perhaps to keep the secret from falling into enemy hands), though he indicates he used the same principle behind the work of the common shepherd and sheepdog: ensuring the dog understands that it must run forward at its handler's command and herd sheep. The crucial task emerging from this was focusing the dog's natural desire to assist its human guardian in return for a reward. Donovan's training methods could not have been as labor- or time-intensive as those devised by Colonel Richardson at the dog training camp at Shoeburyness, simply because the sergeant did not have the necessary leisure, and there is no evidence (at least per Rohan) that Donovan had any formal dog-handling training. Yet despite all these odds, Donovan and Rags taught each other just what needed doing in the erratic, symbiotic schoolroom of the battlefield, discovering in each other the helper and friend each never knew he needed.[6]

Rohan suggests that Donovan first framed what he wanted Rags to learn by doing it himself: he simply ran past Rags, over and over again, with a piece of paper in his mouth. He then put the paper between Rags's own teeth and called him. After doing this a number of times, Donovan "called the dog to him after another soldier had placed a folded paper in Rags's teeth," Rohan writes. "Eventually he taught Rags that when a paper was given to him he was to bring it to Donovan, and that when Donovan placed a paper in Rags's teeth and said, 'Go find,' the dog was to carry it toward the guns until he found someone who would take it from him."[7] Rags saw that by doing these things, he gained praise from Donovan and from the other men. This was the desideratum to a dog as serious about his work as Rags was, and it would succeed in training him under circumstances quite foreign to Colonel Richardson's standard. (Rags would also circumvent another of the colonel's hard and fast rules. Colonel Richardson pointed out in his guide to the training of messenger dogs that "I have rarely found a dog with a gaily carried tail, which curled over its back or sideways, of any value," because this tail denoted "a certain levity of character." Obviously, Rags's own curling tail, that possible inheritance from a poodle ancestor, proved neither the colonel's maxim nor a hazard in the carrying out of his tasks and was one part of Rags's body never known to have sustained an injury in battle.)

Colonel Richardson knew a great deal about dogs and how to train them. Yet his strict rules didn't seem to allow for the inborn intelligence that could assist a smart dog and smart handler, like Rags and Donovan, in circumventing formal training standards, as was the case with a later war dog, Smoky. A Yorkshire terrier weighing four pounds, Smoky was found in 1944 by an American soldier in a foxhole in New Guinea and later sold to Corporal William Wynne of the Fifth Air Force, Twenty-Sixth Photo Recon Squadron. Smoky seemed moved by gratitude toward her soldier to serve, and she was capable of great acts of heroism. During the Luzon campaign, Smoky carried telegraph wire through a seventy-foot-long drainage pipe under an airfield too exposed to enemy fire to safely allow men to dig. Thanks to Smoky's help, soldiers' lives were saved, and later, as the world's first therapy dog, she helped soldiers heal from less tangible wounds.

The truth is, whatever the proven effectiveness of Colonel Richardson's dispatch dogs, some, like Smoky and Rags, were just born to be the war dogs they became.[8] And Donovan, described by Rohan as an uncomplicated, practical, and heartfelt son of the Midwest, was one of those men who, like Corporal Wynne, was born to rescue and train his dog to be a successful participant in battle. What Rags and Donovan had could arguably be called a match made in heaven and tested in hell.

One hot July day outside the quaint Picardy town of Laversine, Rags's impromptu training was put to its first serious test.

While Donovan was out on patrol, Rags had been befriended by a private whom Rohan calls Welch. Welch enjoyed Rags and spent his free time petting and feeding him and taking Rags's attention off Donovan's absence, even as Rags probably helped take Welch's mind off battles to come. Laversine is a little under ten miles west of Soissons and might be thought to have been at negligible risk of shellfire, though as John Ellis writes, "the big guns were usually trained on reserve and rear areas" so as to avoid near misses too close to their own lines.[9] According to Rohan, Private Welch was with Rags when a stray shell fell virtually beside them. This shell may have been an 88 mm "whizz-bang." As feared for its silent approach as for its lethal force, it may not have been audible even to Rags until the last minute. Clearly Welch did not hear it, because while Rohan says the explosion left Rags unharmed, Welch suffered serious shrapnel wounds. Under such conditions, most dogs would have run away. That is what the superbly courageous Don, the collie-shepherd mascot of the Twenty-Third Regiment had done, and nobody blamed him for it. But Rags did not flee; he went searching for Donovan. Finding some artillerymen instead, he barked at them until they followed him back to where Welch lay. Rohan implies that Welch later died. But had Rags not sought help for him, Welch could have suffered a more miserable death in the shell crater than in a field hospital back of the front line.[10]

By helping Welch, Rags had taken on another specialized job for which intensive training was the norm. Locating and assisting the wounded was usually the responsibility of Red Cross "mercy dogs," animals specifically trained to find and bring aid to battlefield casualties.

These dogs were fitted with saddlebags of first-aid supplies to treat injuries in the field before the wounded were stretchered to the sector infirmary. "On finding victims, the dogs were trained to return to their handler carrying their leash in a certain way, or even bearing a helmet or piece of uniform, so as to alert the medics that a man needed help."[11]

From Welch's tragedy, Rags learned another lesson that would help save the lives of other soldiers.

As many down the years would discover, a striking and unchanging characteristic of Rags was his sudden habit of wandering away from any place where he lived. Sometimes when he was unhappy or bothered by crowds, or just from his inveterate curiosity, he would simply take off. Whatever the reason, on this particular day—maybe Donovan had left him alone for too long—Rags abandoned the encampment. Somewhere out in no-man's-land, picking his way around shell craters, he found a dead runner. To say that these men performed a job nobody in their right mind would want to do is putting it lightly. When just lifting your head over the top of a trench could get it blown off, actually standing upright, albeit running like hell across a torn landscape where you were the only moving target for the superb marksmen of the German army, seemed an insane employment even for the fastest sprinter. But every army has its warriors of larger-than-life courage and larger-than-life bravado (sometimes both at the same time), and there were many of these among the runners on both sides of the battle. The British and the Germans both used messenger dogs as well as runners, but without a service dog program, the Americans had to rely on men to dash across no-man's-land under gunfire and, hopefully, like the British dispatch dog Major, dance between the bullets. But everyone in the United States Army Signal Corps knew and took risks: throughout all branches of the signal corps, to whom runners belonged, casualties were very high, second in numbers only to those incurred by front-line infantry.[12]

Sniffing around the dead runner's body, Rags located a piece of paper, either still clenched in the man's hand or pinned to his blouse, as was the custom. Rohan says that Rags plucked up the note and hurried with it back to find Donovan. The note was written by an officer whose unit was surrounded near the Soissons–Paris road. Headquarters had been frantically trying to contact the unit to determine their status.

Rohan gives the text of the message: "I have forty-two men, mixed, healthy, and wounded. We have advanced to the road, but can go no farther. Most of the men are from the Twenty-sixth Infantry. I am the only officer. Machine-guns at our rear, front, right, and left. Send infantry officer to take command. I need machine-gun ammunition."[13] The Twenty-Sixth Infantry's officers had taken a terrible blow. Of its ninety-six officers, "twenty were killed and forty-two were wounded" in this battle, writes the regimental adjutant who authored *The Twenty-Sixth Infantry in France*. This sounds like the situation described by Capt. Shipley Thomas in a 1976 interview. Lieutenant Thomas was an intelligence officer who, with Capt. Barnwell Rhett Legge, would be saved by Rags's efforts during the Meuse-Argonne offensive. On July 22, during the Soissons offensive, Thomas recalled that he and Captain Legge were the only officers left: "Our colonel is dead, our lieutenant colonel is dead, and all the majors are dead or wounded," much like the Twenty-Sixth Infantry men described in the note Rags found.[14] "The regiment came out under the command of a Captain of less than two years experience," *The Twenty-Sixth Infantry in France* continues, "and one battalion was commanded by a First Lieutenant."[15] Perhaps this first lieutenant was the officer who sent the note intercepted by Rags.

Rohan says Donovan cut into a wire and called the message in to the artillery post, but he doesn't state whether the unit was able to escape their trap. What is clear is that by retrieving and delivering a fragile slip of paper from a dead man's hand, Rags gave an officer and his men at least a fighting chance for survival.

Located some twenty miles south of Verdun, the town of Saint-Mihiel, with its ancient Benedictine abbey and quaint red-tiled houses, had been in German hands since 1914. Most of the contested landscape since 1914, from north to south, was low-lying and utterly unsuitable for defense, so that "the most trivial little bump in the ground . . . became an important strategic point."[16]

What made Saint-Mihiel a particularly painful headache for Allied forces was that though it was not particularly high-lying, it jutted into territory not held by Germany, giving its enemy occupiers a surprisingly durable tactical advantage. "It was considered advisable," states the

Seventh Field Artillery history, "to take St Mihiel, straightening out the battle line and thereby remove the constant danger of a flank attack on Verdun," that bloody sector that had devoured so many soldiers' lives two years earlier.[17]

On July 23, the day after the battle of Soissons was over, "French trucks conveyed the foot troops as rapidly as possible to the Saizerais sector in Lorraine on the left of the Moselle River," wrote Gen. Charles P. Summerall in his memoirs. There, the First Division relieved the Second Moroccan Division from then until the first part of August. The foot troops were followed by the artillery, which is what brought Donovan and Rags along with the Seventh Field Artillery to that location. Between "frequent bombardments and several raids in which a few prisoners were taken and men killed and wounded," Summerall wrote, the division conducted training sessions, leaves were granted within the sector, and there was delousing and issuing of clean uniforms to all the men.[18]

During this relatively quiet time, which lasted until the division moved on to Vaucouleurs for training on August 23–24, Donovan added more skills to Rags's repertoire. According to Rohan, "Rags expanded his knowledge of English, improved his message-carrying technique," and memorized what could be termed the only trick he ever deigned to perform. This was a salute, or as close an approximation to one as a dog could be taught to perform. Donovan taught Rags not only to sit back on his haunches and lift a paw toward his right eye but to do so whenever he saw soldiers saluting.[19]

This salute was no passing fancy, to be forgotten over time. Over ten years later and in another country, whenever he saw soldiers on parade, Rags would still lift his paw just as Donovan had trained him to do.

Moving on with the troops to Vaucouleurs, Donovan and Rags went back to work, scouting and patching lines. It was here that Rags learned the difference between broken and unbroken wire. The French telegraphy technology adopted by the American signal corps used insulated wire laid down side by side with grounding spikes at the ends. Between the wires was an induction set powered by batteries. This transmitting station sent buzzer signals over the line. Did Rags notice the difference between live, vibrating wires and dead ones that were ruptured? Or did he do his work by sight, understanding that when a wire was taut and connected, it was good, and when it was loose and frayed, it meant he and his guardian had to venture out under fire to repair it? However they functioned, Rags's powers of concentration and discernment were obviously formidable. Soon, he was an indispensable assistant to Donovan. "Rags expedited Donovan's work," writes Rohan. He would run alongside a wire, and when he found a break, he would sit down and bark until Donovan came to where he was. Rags was especially effective in the sector's thick fog, when human eyes and ears were of no use whatsoever.[20]

It is possible that Rags was tracking one of these communications wires too far when he got separated from Donovan. This happened just at the time the Seventh Artillery was on the move toward Saint-Mihiel; for Rags, the world was all confusion again. Unable to find Donovan, he rejoined the other First Division men. "Rags stuck with the guns and rode the caissons as they bumped over the roads" toward Vaucouleurs, which lay some twenty miles south of Saint-Mihiel. "The terrier was forced to fend for himself as the First Division moved up for the St. Mihiel push," wrote Rohan.[21] This is not to say Rags had no friends in the division or that he didn't make new ones. As he had done with the artillery, somewhere along the way Rags attached himself to a couple of reconnaissance men, other members of the signal corps. These men were not like Donovan, however, running along with a coil of wire over one shoulder (or a reel hanging off his back) and a field set dangling from the other. These soldiers sat in the basket of a sausage-shaped surveillance balloon, still tethered to the ground, and it was there that Rohan says they gave Rags a bite of their lunch. When it was time for them to go up, Rags was still in the basket.

According to Rohan, who again may have based his account on eyewitness testimony, Rags made no move to leave and, in fact, slept soundly as the basket floated aloft. The men let him rest as they recorded enemy positions from the edges of the swaying basket. It is no wonder Rags should have been so relaxed, albeit in the strangest circumstances of his military career to date. Floating high above the tortured landscape and its swarms of struggling men, horses, and machines, he may have enjoyed the most noiseless half hour in his life.

As always, for Rags the calm was brief. An enemy airplane, a Fokker, appeared from out of nowhere, its buzzing whine intercut by antiaircraft guns blasting at it from the ground. In turn, the pilot began firing at the balloon. The observers kept taking notes and telephoning the information until their lines were cut by bullets, which, with a punctured balloon that was rapidly deflating, left them little sane reason to be a thousand feet in the air with a German fighter plane approaching.

The men readied their parachutes, one took Rags under an arm, and out they jumped. As the men and Rags floated down, Rohan says the Fokker returned. The plane was diving straight for them when the German pilot could be seen sticking his head out of the cockpit, as if to confirm what he couldn't believe he was seeing. Pulling back on the throttle, the pilot was seen to grin below his goggles, wave, and then bank off in the opposite direction. However much this enemy pilot may have wanted to blast these Americans conveniently out of the sky, this would have meant killing the little dog gallantly barking his head off under the recon man's arm.

Rags came to earth to face his master, Donovan, who now had a new responsibility on his hands. When a squad leader was cut down by a bullet, Donovan volunteered to take his place. He handed his telephone equipment over to other signal corpsmen and was soon leading nine men, rifle, ammunition, and grenades ready, crouching low to the ground or crawling under the thorny vines of rusted barbed wire, into enemy territory. Donovan had again tried to leave Rags behind, Rohan says, but, as ever, his efforts were to no avail. So alongside the squad leader trotted an intrepid canine doughboy with a gaily carried tail.

And again, Rags's acts belied that cheerful appendage. Donovan had captured an enemy Howitzer but did not know how to fire it, so he got Rags to run back to the artillery with a note asking for help. This was Rags's first opportunity to carry a message, and he did it without a hitch. It was a testament to Rags's ability to deliver a message to the right man and get the results desired. It was also a promising dress rehearsal for what was to come.

Rohan claims that during Donovan's temporary service with the infantry, Rags even had an experience of hand-to-hand fighting, because by this point it was clear that the terrier could not abide

Germans. Though most mascots were loyal, occasionally some would switch sides, depending on the quality of victuals or treatment offered by the erstwhile enemy. A famous example was an Alsatian sheepdog named Tommy, who began with the Germans and ended up with a regiment of Canadian Scots. Wounded in the shoulder and blinded in one eye, Tommy seemed to enjoy sitting outside the American Red Cross headquarters in Paris showing off the Croix de Guerre he had been awarded for meritorious service.[22]

Rags was not a dog to cross battle lines so effortlessly. He had taken a decided dislike to the kaiser's troops, says Rohan, openly snarling at prisoners in German uniform much as, later in life in America, he would bare his teeth at civilian males while greeting uniformed soldiers with wagging tail.

A group of Germans surprised by Donovan's squad went on the attack, and though barely visible in the dust and smoke at their booted feet as they grappled with the Americans between the zigzag walls of a trench, "Rags tried to nip one of them who was pressing Donovan hard," says Rohan. Rags bit into the man's boot and held on, though the German tried to shake him off. Rags's effort, if it really occurred, was like that of Smoky, quite small when seen against the huge picture of the war, yet seriously effective in her own way. By distracting the enemy, Rags played a part in the strategy that shifted the conflict in the Americans' favor. "The [German] trench was taken," wrote Rohan. "The American advance swept on." Rohan then says that Rags came again to Donovan's aid by clamping his teeth into the wrist of a German soldier who had attacked Donovan in hand-to-hand combat.[23]

Whether any of this actually happened—or whether, as Rohan describes, Rags yet again leaped to Donovan's defense in a wrestling match to which the sergeant had challenged a German officer who had kicked the terrier—there were clearly enough of these accounts in the air years after the war to point to some kind of active engagement on Rags's part in scenarios that always involve Donovan, man helping dog, dog helping man.

In reality, however, Rags need not have worked so hard. Through two exhausting battles, he had made quite a favorable impression on just about everyone he met, officers and men alike. One of them was the "Old Man" himself, General Summerall.

Appointed chief of the First Division on July 17, 1918, Charles P. Summerall was fifty-one years old and at the top of his game, a leader about whom his men were known to say lovingly, "Summerall may be a son-of-a-bitch, but he's our son-of-a-bitch." A hardscrabble boyhood in the post–Civil War South and a gentle, educated, and incredibly brave mother formed a man with sensitive eyes and obdurate will who became the model for a perfectionism for which soldiers loved or hated him. Like General Pershing, Summerall could be impossibly demanding. But he cared about his men, visiting them in the trenches, writing personal letters to bereaved families, paying as much attention to the details of a soldier's welfare as he did to whether a tunic was neatly buttoned.

Summerall also cared about horses and mules used in battle, a concern that went back almost twenty years. Summerall was with the American troops who marched on Beijing in the summer of 1900 to rescue besieged American and European diplomats and their families during the Boxer Uprising. Summerall turned his guns on the ancient gates of the Forbidden City; the Manchu imperial family having fled, he enjoyed touring elegant and mysterious pavilions never before seen by a foreigner. Yet in his memoirs, he devoted almost equal space to the heroism of his artillery battery's draft horse Putnam (later renamed Peking), who alone pulled a heavy gun up a steep slope outside Beijing. To Summerall, who had himself persevered against all odds, Putnam was as much a hero as any of the men. In 1918 France, while visiting the trenches, he scrutinized how the horses were treated, whether they were fed, watered, and as comfortable as could be expected under the circumstances. When they were not, Summerall did more than shake his head in regret. He lit fires under those whose negligence had caused the suffering of animals who did so much for the war effort and deserved better thanks for it.[24]

The day Summerall and Rags crossed paths—Rohan says it was August 11, 1918—the general was probably thinking mostly about the upcoming assault on the Saint-Mihiel salient, scheduled for a month hence. Rags had been in the general's vicinity not to meet such a celebrity but, as Rohan points out, more likely due to the distraction of pleasant aromas wafting from the post of command mess kitchen. Rags was seen to trot over to the general, sit in front of him, and lift a paw in the salute Donovan had taught him. When Summerall seemed not to notice, Rags barked. "Hello," said the general. "You look as if you were trying to salute. What can we do for you?"[25]

Donovan seems to have been amused but thought nothing more of this, Rohan tells us, and brought Rags back to his unit. But as soon as he and Rags rejoined the signal corps, the men exclaimed at the sight of them, having assumed they had both been killed. When Donovan explained that he had been ordered to serve with the infantry, one of the men laughed. "The skipper," as he called Summerall, had had a few things to say about making cannon fodder of a good signalman. Donovan expressed pleasure that "the Old Man" actually took such a personal interest in his welfare. "He wasn't worryin' about you," Rohan has the other man retort. "He don't want nothin' to happen to Rags."[26]

5

Last Battle

Second Lt. (later Gen.) George Catlett Marshall, famous for reorganizing war-torn Europe after World War II, was given a small taste in the battlefields of 1918 France of what was to come a quarter century into his future.

Before the Saint-Mihiel offensive had even started, Marshall was given the monumental task of transporting troops from the Saint-Mihiel sector to the Meuse-Argonne, a region held by the Germans since 1914 and scored by trenches and barbed wire–wreathed defensive lines. With barely time for rest, Lieutenant Marshall had to move men, animals, cook wagons, and matériel along transport routes that were impossible at best. As he wrote in his memoirs, "I could not recall an incident in history where the fighting of one battle had been preceded by the plan for a later battle to be fought by the same army on a different front."[1]

Historian Edward Lengel puts the task Marshall had to do and the terrain and circumstances in which he had to do it into detailed perspective: "Three dirt roads and three light railways bore the traffic of fifteen divisions and three corps headquarters."[2] Marshall himself notes in his memoirs that he was at Toul on the Moselle River the night these thousands of men, animals, and machines were on the move to Ligny, a fifty-mile stretch, and on going out to inspect he saw that the entire road was solid with traffic, creeping along in pitch darkness. Marshall could only shake his head that there were not more accidents en route than there already were.[3]

General Pershing had hoped that Saint-Mihiel might have been just the beginning of a larger assault to push on to the city of Metz, almost forty miles to the northeast. The backbone of the German army's rail transport system was located there, and he wanted to break it. French marshal Ferdinand Foch, on the other hand, had argued that Pershing

41

should cut back on or abandon his Saint-Mihiel push and move west toward the Meuse-Argonne region. Pershing refused to do this, and the survivors of Saint-Mihiel must have groaned when told they were to enter another battle just after the first one ended. They were allowed only five days' rest in the Bois de la Belle Ozière. Then, on September 20, the regiment was ordered to proceed northwest across the freshly captured Saint-Mihiel salient in what was optimistically called a "big push."[4] By September 29, the Americans had established themselves near Charpentry, and from there, a five-mile drive northwest across the Meuse River, they planned to jump off at the hilly little town of Exermont on October 4.[5]

Rohan writes that this "big push" had left Donovan and Rags behind, but somehow, through the vast traffic jam, they rejoined the Seventh Field Artillery in the area around Serieux farm. There, the regiment's post of command had been transferred to the cellar of the house. These French farms played as crucial a role in the war as the various *côtes*, or hills, around them on which enemy emplacements bristled. The often-bombed-out structures were nowhere near the comparative luxury of German officers' trench dwellings, in which Allied soldiers would be amazed to find everything from wooden floors and carpets to wallpaper and framed pictures, a battlefield approximation of beloved German *Gemütlichkeit*. But these French farmhouse ruins made excellent, if exposed, dugouts for headquarters, the more so because of their construction and shape. "The farms here are fortresses in themselves," noted British officer Alexander Gillespie toward the war's end. They were built around a courtyard, "the middle of which forms a manure heap, the size of which I never saw equalled in any part of the world." It was a drawback one had to endure in exchange for the protection of the farm's thick stone walls and deep basement.[6]

A stuccoed two-story country house with classical pilasters and pediment, Ferme de Serieux looks today as if it never endured any sound above the buzzing of bees in wildflowers, but it was hardly so quiet in the fall of 1918; in fact, the house had been a target of German attacks from the first day the post was established there. In a sample of what a given day at the Twenty-Sixth Infantry post of command might deliver, an officer and his staff were eating their lunch in the cellar (where the regimental kitchen had been set up) when enemy artillery lobbed three shells into the vicinity. One fell short, the second overshot the mark, and the third sadly killed the horses hitched to a supply wagon, wounding a soldier nearby and rendering him helpless in the exposed courtyard. One didn't have to be a shining lieutenant or battle-hardened sergeant to be a hero. "With entire disregard for his own safety," stated the historian of the Twenty-Sixth Infantry, "Cook Lee rushed to the aid of the wounded man and pulled him to shelter." Cook Lee was not the only hero of these early days of the Meuse-Argonne push: the Seventh Field Artillery history also singles out the Regimental Telephone Detail for special kudos. The detail "rendered wonderful service during this offensive," the historian explains. "The linemen in the face of severe fighting and difficult terrain kept constant communication with the Second Infantry Brigade Headquarters and the two Battalion Headquarters of the Seventh."[7] Donovan was part of that "wonderful service," and so was Rags. By running ahead to where Donovan couldn't go and barking when he found a break in a line, Rags was the sergeant's very own secret weapon in the war.[8]

And Rags proved his worth again not long after the Seventh Artillery began setting up for the Meuse-Argonne offensive. During one of his and Donovan's joint patrols repairing wire, they stumbled over the body of a runner.

As with the runner Rags had found earlier, this man still had his message on his person. Donovan read it and, as Rohan writes, instantly saw its implications:

From C.O. First Btn. 26th Infantry:
Oct 2—12:30 p.m.:
To Captain [Shipley] Thomas, Intelligence Officer:
Have artillery that is firing in small oblong-shaped woods, directly in front and on right of first objective, lengthen range and pound hell out of woods. Machine-gun nests are located there.
[Capt. Barnwell Rhett] Legge, cdg.[9]

Donovan cut into one wire after another in an effort to relay the message to the artillery, but none was live. Rags was wearing his gas mask, so Donovan had to tie the message around his neck—an unfamiliar procedure for a dog who had always carried messages in his mouth and a rehearsal for what was to come in the next few days. Soldiers themselves were often so hampered by their gas masks that they risked taking them off to be able to see where they were and what they (and the enemy) were doing. Rohan asserts how much Rags loathed his mask, which, being home-made, was likely even more uncomfortable than the bespoke versions made for British and European dispatch dogs and equines. Yet despite this handicap, Rags started toward the rear, to where the guns were, and the message got delivered.

Rohan says he could never identify the person who received the message Rags carried to the artillery. (The man may not have survived the war to tell the tale.) But the scrap of paper was on file, proof that a call for help had gone out and that it had been acted upon. Thanks to Rags, wrote Rohan, the artillery let fly with enough shells to light up the wooded area concealing the machine gunners, allowing the infantry to proceed to their task.[10]

This was not Rags's only assistance to the Twenty-Sixth at this time. As Rohan wrote, "The Twenty-Sixth Infantry was driving through the valley, between Hills 272 and 269, after the Ferme d'Arietal had fallen." They had been ordered to enter the woods (the Bois de Moncy) on the other side of the valley "until stopped at dusk by strong resistance from resting enemy machine guns and artillery on Hill 272."[11] While the Twenty-Sixth was held up in the woods, they had sent a patrol that afternoon up to Hill 263; these men took the rise handily, but only just managed to keep it. From the hill, "they announced that if someone would give them a brigade, they would 'clean out the whole business' that evening."[12] Though the Seventh Field Artillery tried to protect the men with a box barrage (several barrages isolating a position from enemy attack), the Germans had the Americans in their sights and began a counteroffensive. This in turn destroyed communications wire, the infantry's lifeline to the artillery. "A runner was started rearward," says Rohan.[13] The artillery was positioned some four hundred yards away, relatively close in battlefield terms. But they were not close enough; the runner was cut down midway. This occurred not far from where Rags and Donovan were.

Rags dashed out to where the runner lay, then led Donovan back to the corpse. Donovan retrieved the man's message, memorized it, and telephoned the instructions on to the artillery. "Soon, the seventy-fives of the Seventh were crashing their shells into the wood" and at Hill 272, from which heavy fire poured a firestorm. By 8:30 on the foggy morning of October 9, "with howitzers pounding Hill 272," the Sixteenth Infantry took the hill at last, capturing in the process dozens of German machine guns positioned up and down the slopes. Rags had done his bit for the Sixteenth, a favor that was to be remembered well seven years down the road.[14]

The American commanders rejoiced that they and the Allies were finally overtaking long-held German positions. However, as they edged their way into what had been German territory for three years, riddled with bunkers, trenches, traps, and the ever-present barbed wire, they were also moving farther away from their posts of command and thus from the communications centers. The increased distance meant having to station at intervals more linemen, signalmen, and runners, "four to five men at a post," according to the Seventh Field Artillery history.[15] For this battle, writes Maj. Douglas J. Orsi, "the Division axis of liaison would be kept separate from the regimental wire system; the infantry brigade would be connected to its regiments on a separate wire system," which connected at the infantry brigade post of command. What this did, besides saving wire (the American forces would end the fighting on November 11 with only a five-day supply remaining), was space signal teams more evenly, allowing for fewer glitches in the system caused by too much distance between stations. "Another change [from the battle of Soissons] was that message centers were now organized at the PC of the division, brigades and infantry regiments, and they maintained all means of communicating with higher headquarters," Orsi explains. There was a clear intention of letting no information go astray or sit around because of poor communications conditions or a commander's absence or his failure to keep higher command constantly informed. This obsession with keeping communications as intact and viable as possible does much to explain Donovan's efforts—even to the point of self-sacrifice—to carry messages through to the artillery.[16]

The Seventh Field Artillery's new post of command lay near the lower southeast slope of Hill 212, a small rise in the rolling terrain that lay a little over a mile to the rear of the action. Donovan and Rags, like the other signalmen, patrolled their appointed sectors, repairing breaks, testing lines, and phoning in information as it came. When there came a lull in the fighting, Rohan says that Donovan, who had finished repairs, used the opportunity to find a shell crater to lie down in for a rest with Rags. But theirs was a short siesta.

"Without any preliminary ranging shots," says Rohan, referring to a gunner's tactic of probing a sector to determine the location of a target, "the enemy seemed to concentrate every gun on this little patch of ground." As Gen. George Marshall noted, it was no easy thing for artillery to destroy communications wire, "at best a tedious process," he wrote. It was estimated, he explained, "that five hundred shots from a 75 [mm gun] were necessary to cut a gap five meters wide and ten meters long."[17] Evidently the German gunners decided to let fly with all the ordnance they possessed in hopes that one or two shells would smash American and Allied communications.

What apparently puzzled Donovan was that his own artillery had not responded with return fire. Rohan says Donovan pulled up some wire that had fallen into his shell crater and cut into it with his field set to see what was going on. He found himself in the middle of a distress call from a front-line officer who was trying to raise the Seventh Artillery. The Second Brigade (the Twenty-Sixth and Twenty-Eighth Infantry regiments) had taken Hill 263 not long after the Sixteenth Infantry had seized Hill 272.[18] As darkness fell, the doughboys "hung on" despite the fact that "the hilltop had become a seething inferno." The Germans were letting off flanking fire, "which seemed at times to be coming almost from the rear," with heavy losses among the men.[19]

The officer needed the artillery to focus firepower on the German position; only by cutting off this barrage could he save his men from being blasted completely off the hill. Since the wire did not allow Donovan to transmit the message on to the rear (a complicating feature of the telephone system then in use), he wrote the information down and, as Rohan wrote, "he promised to try to get the message through." Based on what happened next, we may take it that Donovan planned either to transmit the message via an intact wire farther up, should he find one, or to just run the message back to the post of command—either way, the risks were about even. Picking up Rags, Donovan began to sprint toward the rear. Stopping to repair a break and test the connection, he smelled poison gas. Rags was already wearing his gas mask; Donovan donned his and moved on. He was actually rather close to his post of command, "within perhaps half a kilometer of the Seventh Field Artillery," estimated Rohan.[20]

Though the Germans' curtain of fire continued its approach, Donovan didn't stop working on the line. Then, when it looked suicidal to continue, and there was no time for him to run the message through himself, he turned to the far smaller, faster Rags. It was time to see whether all that training in the quiet sectors would pay off in this ear-splitting firestorm, and he had every reason to doubt that it would. Such conditions were known to try the nerves of even formally trained dispatch dogs; Signaller Bert Chaney of the 117th London Regiment recalled trying to send not one but two messenger dogs into the thick of shellfire, as there was no other way of calling up reinforcements. The first dog ran back to Chaney, "scared out of its wits," he wrote, while the second "dropped flat on his stomach and there was no shifting him."[21]

Donovan didn't have the leisure to worry about how Rags would do. He just had to get him sent off and hope for the best. So, tying his message to Rags's collar with a piece of telephone wire, Donovan pushed the terrier back toward the artillery, following him at close quarters along the wire so that Rags would be assured that all was well. And they would likely have made it safely together, had the luck that had been theirs since Soissons not chosen this moment to fail.

As dog and man scrambled across the broken ground, a sudden blast sent them sprawling. The close-range explosion was so severe that it tore off Rags's and Donovan's gas masks, exposing both to the deadly fumes. Rags suffered shrapnel wounds to his right forepaw and his right ear and blinding in his right eye (later attributed to gas exposure rather than shrapnel).[22] He had also inhaled gas, starting the cough that would trouble him the rest of his life. Donovan took the harsh brunt of the blast, taking shrapnel wounds to his arms and legs. Worse, he too had suffered gas exposure. Yet he roused himself enough to send Rags off again toward the guns.[23]

Limping across the shattered ground, Rags didn't make it far before another blast knocked him sideways. Getting up, he started again; another explosion sent him rolling into a shell crater, where he fell straight into the arms of a liaison officer taking shelter there. "Tucking the still gasping Rags under his arm," wrote Rohan, "the man raced rearward to the foot of Hill 212," dodging shellfire along the way. Just as Rags and the officer reached shelter, someone found Donovan crawling up the escarpment and carried him in. It was at this point that the message was taken off Rags's collar and delivered to Col. (later Brig. Gen.) Lucius R. Holbrook.[24]

Holbrook may have already known Donovan and perhaps Rags, too: he had spent several years in the Philippines at the same time Donovan was there and in France had commanded the Seventh Field Artillery until August. The night Rags and Donovan were carried in, as luck would have it, Holbrook was in charge of the First Field Artillery Brigade, of which the Seventh Artillery formed a part.

Donovan's message, brought by Rags through the barrage, was shortly relayed to the artillery. Donovan, who was coming to, was heard to mumble one question, about whether "the dog" had survived. But when he heard the guns boom, he said, "Good ol' Rags. He made it."[25] As the earth trembled, Donovan and Rags were put on a stretcher, per Colonel Holbrook's orders. "Get some men and take the sergeant and this dog to a dressing-station," he said. "Tell them the dog is to get the same treatment as a soldier."[26]

For Donovan and for Rags, this war was over. Another lay ahead: that of staying together as much as staying alive.

The latter was enough of a challenge. Rohan tells of how the ambulance in which Donovan was being transported to the first field hospital came under fire as an aviator came out of nowhere and "emptied a machine belt" at the speeding vehicle. "Donovan and Rags were on the top 'shelf' of that ambulance," Rohan wrote. "An airplane bullet plugged through the roof, tore between Donovan's feet, and killed the soldier on the bottom stretcher." The bullet likely missed Rags by mere inches, since he was often at the foot of Donovan's bed.[27]

This would qualify for miracle status, but so did something equally important: that Donovan and Rags were able to remain a unit, always together, on stretchers and cots. Donovan was in no state to inform people about Rags and why he was with him. Yet each time Rags was on the point of being ejected from Donovan's bed, someone who knew him or knew about him stepped in to straighten things out. In fact, Rags's story had begun to take on a life of its own; it now began to take hold in the memories and consciousness of those who had not even fought alongside him.

Thus at the field hospital, the ambulance men had to explain that Rags was with Donovan per instructions from field headquarters. These instructions, originally Colonel Holbrook's, were now interpreted to mean they had issued straight from General Summerall himself. The general, after all, had been seen to take an interest in Rags's welfare after Soissons. And it was obvious that the dog, like the man, had also suffered wounds in battle. In any case, even if the hospital commander or a doctor chose to question the dog's presence, it meant taking the risk of contacting Summerall himself and appearing to question what he had ordered—and Summerall was not known to take kindly to such overtures. It was at this hospital, where Rags lay under Donovan's cot, that Rags's wounds were finally tended and re-dressed. His nutritional needs were also taken in hand by a nurse who spoon-fed him the same broth prepared for the patients.[28]

Donovan was then moved to the base hospital, where the same line of enquiry arose about a dog in the ward. This time, however, the doctor in charge proved to need little convincing. A lover of dogs, he took time to perform minor surgery on Rags, removing shrapnel shards from his face. When it came time to transport Donovan to the train for his final French destination, a large hospital set up in a monastery, this doctor made sure to inform the next set of ambulance men about Rags and those orders from headquarters.[29]

Those "orders" were in turn relayed to the commander in charge of the hospital train, who abided by them strictly. "For two days and nights they rode the train," says Rohan, "sometimes crawling snail-like, now and then sidetracked for munitions, expresses, and at intervals tearing along at top speed to clear the track for troops and supplies." By the time the wounded were taken off and transported to the monastery, the medical officer in charge there had been informed of the "orders from headquarters," which he took to mean from the pen of General Pershing himself. Thanks to this officer, Rags was seen to by a professional veterinarian.[30]

Throughout the days and weeks Donovan was a patient at the monastery, Rags slept under his cot, rarely venturing far (he was not encouraged to wander through the wards, as there were still those who might report him). From time to time, Rags was able to see his master. Rohan was told that a ward nurse would lift Rags up and place him next to Donovan, who appreciated seeing that the dog was well. Whenever Rags got excited and vocal at seeing Donovan, the latter assured the nurse that all she had to do was hush him quietly. It was a tactic that always worked as promised.[31]

Unlike Donovan, Rags improved rapidly. By Armistice Day in November, he was able to get outside the hospital ward, where he had more freedom to roam as he loved to do. And he occasionally got into scrapes. Once Rags had an altercation with the billy goat of a herd kept by the hospital to provide milk for the patients. Another time, while sitting beside a stream admiring the flowing water, Rags saw an eel, which he tried to fish out. He ended up in the water with it and had to be rescued. And of course, he once again had an altercation with a cat, this one not a stray, but a kitten bought by the patients as a gift for a nurse who had lost her son in battle. When Rags and the kitten did meet, the latter struck him on the nose with her paw and fled the ward, leaving the terrier to crawl back under the safety of Donovan's bed.[32]

It was one thing to keep Rags with Donovan during his time in the monastery hospital, thanks to the tight-knit circles of doctors, nurses, ambulance men, and soldiers, each of whom knew the story of the brave little mutt of Soissons, Saint-Mihiel, and the Argonne. It was another thing to ensure that he remained with a man who in the short term needed specialized medical care in hospital settings that did not welcome dogs as a rule and who, even if he lived, would never be in a position to care for a pet dog. Unlike cats, dogs need walks, too much to expect from a man who might never again rise from his bed.

Donovan's shrapnel wounds were the least of his problems: his lungs were damaged beyond repair. Three varieties of gas were used by both sides during the Great War. There was lachrymator, or tear gas, which irritated eyes, nose, and throat but did not kill as a rule. The deadly agents were the asphyxiate and mustard gases. The asphyxiates (chlorine, phosgene, and diphosgene) worked gruesome effects on the body, particularly moist areas like the eyes, mouth, and lungs. A man could be both permanently blinded and gradually unable to breathe, suffering a slow and nightmarish death. Mustard gas was even worse, because on contact, even with covered skin, it caused huge, painful blisters, it also blinded, and it destroyed the lungs, so that when the effects of the initial exposure were over, the sufferer was prone to bronchial infections, which, in those pre-antibiotic days, were lethal. It appears that it was mustard gas that Donovan and Rags were exposed to—it was in the air the nights of October 8–9 and 9–10, when German forces fired it in retaliation for American gas attacks. During the time Donovan was active in the field, the division gas officer reported over 130 mustard gas casualties.[33] As a mustard gas case, the best thing for Donovan was to ship him out of France to the United States, where he could be treated at Fort Sheridan near Chicago. Fort Sheridan had a reputation for specializing in the treatment of gas and shell-shock cases. At least there, Donovan might have a better chance of recovery.[34]

As for Rags, for a while, the staff at the monastery hospital considered giving him a home with them, though such a "home" would have been scarcely more permanent than living under Donovan's cot. In the end, though, it was determined that Rags would be better off, whatever happened, with the wounded man from whom he could not be parted. So when Donovan was settled into his berth on a hospital train headed for the port of Brest, Rags was in his accustomed place at Donovan's feet, and there he stayed, except for the occasional visit with the other wounded men, many of whom recognized him as "the little pup that took a message through a barrage."[35]

The train finally reached Brest on the coast of Brittany, a sprawling harbor city then still rich with historic buildings that would be destroyed almost entirely by war a quarter of a century later. As one of the more fragile patients on the train, Donovan was transported to the hospital ship via ambulance from the station. As his stretcher was lifted into the waiting vehicle, Rags jumped up, as he was used to doing by now, to join him. "But the ambulance men—replacements who had arrived since the fighting had stopped and had never heard of Rags—unceremoniously pushed him aside and drove away," says Rohan.[36]

There is no great distance from the Gare de Brest to the docks. But Rags had never seen this city before, he was limping on an injured paw, he was blind in one eye. Nonetheless, he somehow followed the ambulance from the train station down to where the ship was waiting. Seeing that Donovan was being carried aboard, Rags tried to follow but was again rebuffed. Rohan writes that when a few First Division patients who were also about to board tried to reason with the medical staff, they were read the rules: army regulations forbade any animals aboard a hospital ship to prevent any infectious diseases being transmitted to immune-compromised patients. To bring a dog on the ship might be a death sentence for the patients and definitely would be a death sentence for the dog.

Even in this hopeless situation Rags was luckier than many dogs, horses, and mules who had served in the Great War. Just as those judged unfit for battle service had been euthanized at the start of the war, at its end many others who had served faithfully were simply left behind by a war machine that could not cope with organizing their return. This pattern was to be repeated in wars over the rest of the twentieth century, down to Vietnam. Still, one of the saddest images of Rags's entire life is not that of him as a forlorn stray on the streets of Paris or ducking shellfire on the battlefields of the Argonne but of him sitting by himself on the edge of the dock in Brest, before him a ship he could not board, beyond it an ocean he could not cross, and behind him a city he didn't know, where his only option was to return to the life of a stray that Donovan and Hickman had rescued him from. Given his battlefield injuries, it is likely he would not have survived very long in the cutthroat world of Brest's back streets.[37]

Among the friends Rags had made on the hospital train was Col. Halstead Dorey. Described as "the most lovable character" his friends ever knew, Dorey, a Missourian, was a West Point graduate. He had served with distinction in the Philippines, where his conciliatory and tolerant treatment of native peoples won their trust despite widespread dislike of the American occupation. After the Great War, Dorey was awarded the Distinguished Service Cross and the Army Distinguished Service Medal for bravery under fire.[38] For being such a redoubtable warrior, Dorey was a man of serene nature and easy humor. And though it was not among the qualities listed in his obituary in 1946, Dorey had just as much compassion as he did courage.

In pain from his injuries but still upright and sprightly, Col. Dorey was being shipped out of France on the same transport as Donovan. Dorey had been one of the wounded officers who recognized Rags on the hospital train as the little hero of the Argonne campaign. Now, spotting Rags on the dock, Dorey told his orderly, "That's Donovan's dog—the one that carried the message through." The decision was made then and there. As coolly as he did everything else, Dorey formulated a plan on the spot. He had his orderly empty one of his bags, lead Rags away from the dock and fit him into the bag, then carry him aboard with the rest of Dorey's luggage, which the colonel presumed (wrongly) nobody would dare search. Within the hour, Rags went from desolation on the Brest docks to comparatively luxurious accommodations (a deck cabin), sequestered under Dorey's bed. He was safe, but only for the moment.[39]

Not long into the voyage, Dorey's stateroom was ordered searched, as were those of the other officers and men. The chief medical officer had gotten wind that there was a pet cat on board, and (rightly) surmised it might not be the only animal on the ship. We may gauge what his response to Rags would have been by considering the fate of this cat. On being located, it was seized, swiftly chloroformed, and tossed overboard. Keeping Rags hidden in a stateroom was problematic enough—had he barked or scratched at the door even once in hearing of someone not in on the secret, he would have joined the unfortunate cat on the bottom of the Atlantic. Rags's past experiences of having to maintain at all times a quiet presence in trenches and hospital wards now stood him in good stead; he was not detected in his dark, cramped hiding place, and Dorey made sure it stayed that way. Rohan says Dorey even raised noisy protest in the chief medical officer's quarters, balancing on his one good leg for emphasis, to such effect that the doctor promised Dorey's stateroom would never again be searched.[40] Yet, incredibly, despite the continued risk, Dorey felt he could hazard taking

Rags down to visit Donovan. The alibi for these visits, which Dorey made with Rags concealed under his greatcoat, was that Donovan had served under Dorey, his company commander, in the Philippines. As the men conversed, the real reason for their meetings peeked a furry face out from Dorey's coat.

In these visits lies another mystery of Rags's extraordinary life: How did Colonel Dorey get away with it? Donovan was not the sole occupant of the hospital ward. Other patients were nearby, not all of whom were unconscious, and there would have been medical staff around from time to time looking after them. Dorey somehow kept Rags a secret from everyone except Donovan. But it is just as possible that Dorey was not alone in this ruse. This is where what Rohan calls "the Rags committee" comes in. As *Stars and Stripes* reported in 1948, after most of those concerned were deceased, "A good portion of the First Division collaborated in getting the dog to Ft. Sheridan, Ill.," past customs (and past quarantine) and on another hospital train heading west, breaking a federal law as well as a few more military ones in the process.[41]

Who these "committee" members were, besides Dorey and his orderly, we may never know. According to Rohan, there was at least one nurse in on the plot as well. From some of these people Rohan may have heard about the furtive meetings at Donovan's bedside—of his emotional reaction to seeing Rags, his admission to Dorey that he did not think he would live long, his worry about what would happen to the terrier when Donovan died. Seeing Donovan's anxiety, Dorey was ready to promise him the moon.

"I'll get Rags on the same train with you," he told Donovan. How that would happen, though, remained a very open question well after the Statue of Liberty came into view.[42]

1. Rags with First Sgt. George Earl Hickman, ca. 1925. This photograph was used for the terrier's 1936 obituary in the *New York Times*. Courtesy the Hon. Raymond G. H. Seitz.

2. (*opposite top*) First Sgt. George Earl Hickman, corescuer of Rags, in training prior to shipping out to Europe, ca. 1917. His love for dogs is evident. Courtesy Claudia Kemmerer Ruibal.

3. (*opposite bottom*) The alert bearing, ears pricked forward, and eyes bright, shown by this unnamed messenger dog from the Great War, outlines every ideal desired by Lt. Col. Edwin H. Richardson, founder of the British war dog training camp at Shoeburyness. Rags, however, always carried his messages in his mouth rather than in the official canister shown here. From Ernest Harold Baynes's *Animal Heroes of the Great War*, 1925.

4. (*above*) Gen. John J. Pershing, commander of U.S. forces, reviews First Division troops with Gen. Charles Pelot Summerall. Pershing and Rags would meet face to face a dozen years after the war. Courtesy Charles P. Summerall IV.

5. (*above*) Fort Sheridan, Illinois, ca. 1925. Rags spent his first year and some months in America here. By permission of the Lake County Discovery Museum, Wauconda, Illinois.

6. (*left*) Col. William N. Bispham, MD, compassionate medical officer of Fort Sheridan, was among those at the fort who looked after Rags following Sergeant Donovan's death. Courtesy the American College of Surgeons, Chicago, Illinois.

7. (*top*) Rags's identification tag, commissioned by his guardian Maj. (later Lt. Col.) Raymond W. Hardenbergh in 1920. Courtesy Jay and Judy Butkus.

8. (*bottom*) Susan Hardenbergh, younger daughter of Maj. and Mrs. Raymond W. Hardenbergh, shown here with Rags on a snowy hill at Governors Island around 1926. Courtesy Jay and Judy Butkus.

9. (*above*) Helen Hardenbergh, daughter of Maj. and Mrs. Raymond W. Hardenbergh, playing with Rags. Courtesy Jay and Judy Butkus.

10. (*opposite top*) Rags at Governors Island, ca. 1929. Courtesy Jay and Judy Butkus.

11. (*opposite bottom*) Rags at Governors Island, watching First Sgt. George Earl Hickman put his platoon through their paces. Rags would often salute the men as they marched past, lifting a paw to his eye, as Sergeant Donovan taught him in France. Courtesy Jay and Judy Butkus.

In the photograph, a partially visible sign reads:

RAGS IS THE ONLY DOG VETERAN WHO WENT
THROUGH THE ENTIRE WORLD WAR AND LIVED
TO TELL THE TALE — IF HE COULD TALK.
GASSED AT MEUSE-ARGONNE
OCT. 9 - 1918
HE AND SERGEANT DONOVAN W...
HIM UP IN PARIS FOR THE FIRST D...
FOUND TOGETHER IN NO-MAN'S LAND—
AND NEARLY DEAD. THE GAS DESTROYE...
LEFT EYE. THE SURGEON WHO RESCU...
WO TOOK THEM BOTH TO THE SAME HO...
LATER ... AME BACK TO THE STAT...
THE S... ...NSPORT DONOVAN SIN...
"GONE...
RAGS ... ...ET HO...
MAJOR R... ...HE IN...
GENERAL'S ... ...ISLA...
MAJOR GIV... ...BUT
CLAIM TO O... ...P.-... ...S B...
TH...TIR...DI...SI...

12. (*above*) Rags with First Sgt. George Earl Hickman in the fall of 1925, preparing for the ill-fated Long Island Kennel Club Dog Show in Brooklyn. Courtesy the Hon. Raymond G. H. Seitz.

13. (*opposite top*) Rags at Fort Hamilton, ca, 1930. Courtesy of the author.

14. (*opposite bottom*) Rags perched precariously atop a cannonball while Brig. Gen. Hugh A. Drum holds him in place. Courtesy the Hon. Raymond G. H. Seitz.

15. Rags at Fort Hamilton in 1925. Seen here are (*extreme left, in light hat*) Dr. Guy Shirey, (*third from left, in dark hat*) Brig. Gen. Robert L. Bullard, Rags, Sgt. George Earl Hickman (holding Rags's lead), Brig. Gen. Charles P. Summerall, and Brig. Gen. Frank Parker. Courtesy the Hon. Raymond G. H. Seitz.

16. Rags and Maj. Raymond W. Hardenbergh examining a check sent to Rags by a young New Yorker in sympathy with him after his public ejection from the Long Island Kennel Club Dog Show, October 1925. Courtesy the Hon. Raymond G. H. Seitz.

17. (*above*) Rags on the only occasion he is known to have given his "pawtograph." At Fort Hamilton in November 1930, he left his paw mark in a copy of Jack Rohan's book *Rags: The Story of a Dog Who Went to War*, which was later sent to the Imperial War Museum in London. (*From left*) Rags's biographer, Jack Rohan; Maj. Raymond W. Hardenbergh; and Brig. Gen. Lucius R. Holbrook. Courtesy the Hon. Raymond G. H. Seitz.

18. (*opposite*) Rags's hurried "signature," using his wounded right paw, as Jack Rohan's lines to the right explain. Courtesy the Imperial War Museum, London.

19. (*right*) A cartoon of Rags created for an advertisement for Jack Rohan's book, ca. 1930. Artist and newspaper unknown. Courtesy Jay and Judy Butkus.

RAGS

THE STORY OF A DOG WHO WENT TO WAR

By Jack Rohan

The ink prints are
the mark made by
Rags with the paw
wounded in action

M C M X X X

NEW YORK AND LONDON

HARPER & BROTHERS PUBLISHERS

20. Rags with the Hardenberghs' new Ford, probably at Fort Hamilton. His thin, aging body can be seen in the reflection in the car door. Courtesy Jay and Judy Butkus.

21. (*top*) Lt. Col. Raymond W. Hardenbergh with Rags, ca. 1935. The mascot is looking all of his nineteen years. Courtesy Jay and Judy Butkus.

22. (*bottom*) Aspin Hill at the start of its existence as a pet cemetery, early 1920s. Courtesy Mary Elizabeth Thurston.

23. Rags's grave at Aspin Hill Memorial Park. Photograph by the author.

24. First Sgt. George Earl Hickman (1890–1962), seen here in middle age. He left behind a collection of lovingly preserved clippings and photographs of First Division Rags, loving him till the end. Courtesy Charles Kemmerer.

25. "The war-worn soldiers of the First Division had room in their hearts for kindness to a homeless little dog," wrote Jack Rohan. The war-worn but courageous little dog felt the same about them. Courtesy the Hon. Raymond G. H. Seitz.

PART 2
Days of Peace

Yet he only asks, with a pleading paw
When this madness of Might shall cease,
To hold in your bosoms one human law—
Remember our dogs in the days of war,
And our dogs in the days of Peace.
—EDWARD PEPLE, "The War Dog" (1918)

6

New World

Unlike many who sailed into New York Harbor as immigrants or visitors or returning citizens, Rags—still homeless and tempest tossed below Colonel Dorey's bed—did not enjoy a first glimpse of the gray-green statue holding her torch beside the golden door.

While the hospital ship lay at anchor for some hours, waiting for a berth, Dorey's orderly had some organizing to do. It was imperative that there be a plan in place for how to get Rags off the ship and on the same train as Donovan without Rags being detected either by military or customs and immigration personnel. Had he been found, Rags would probably have been seized and destroyed.

By the time the ship finally docked and its passengers were being disgorged on foot or via stretcher, Dorey's orderly had worked out a plan. Rags would be secreted off the ship in the same manner in which he had been brought on, in Colonel Dorey's handbag. At the Hoboken railhead, he would be slipped over to another set of First Division men recruited by the orderly using the authority of Dorey. This escort, which was made up of men headed for Fort Sheridan (many of them shell-shock cases), would see to it that Rags and Donovan were on the same train.

A nurse—possibly one who had helped facilitate Dorey's and Rags's visit to Donovan on the ship—colluded with officers who were in on the secret, men whom Dorey had appointed to the now rather populous "Rags committee." Because he was boarding a train that would take him in the opposite direction from the men heading to Chicago, Dorey made a show of wanting to bid them farewell. Despite his leg (and perhaps exaggerating the injury for effect), Dorey made it up the steep steps and onto the west-bound train with Rags concealed under his coat and there handed him over to his new guardians. Dorey was convinced that Rags knew exactly what was going on and that the men who were caring for him could only do so if he stayed hidden and quiet for as long as possible.[1]

And so it was. During the entire trip, Rohan says, Rags crouched quietly under the seat in the train car; even when the engine was changed and shunted with noisy clanks and screeches, the terrier remained still, just as he had done on the hospital ship and, before that, under Donovan's bed at the monastery hospital.[2]

Coming to a stop near Fort Sheridan, over eight hundred miles and a few days later, the train's passengers began to disembark, and Rags's network of friends and caretakers set to work once again. One of the men bunched Rags into his overcoat and then carried the bundle with him off the train under his arm. Rohan says this man was accosted almost immediately by a supervising officer, annoyed that a sick man had his coat off in the chill air. In the middle of this exchange, another soldier approached the captain and diverted his attention by absurdly asking him if he might go into Chicago to visit some friends. As the angry captain yelled that the soldier could do no such thing, the coatless soldier melted with Rags into the surge of the crowd, headed for the main receiving area of Fort Sheridan.[3]

The 1921 United States School of Nursing *Annual* devoted a page of encomium to Fort Sheridan, calling it "one of the most beautiful of the Army posts."[4] It had not always been so. Fort Sheridan dated back to 1670 as a crude trading post for the French, but it was not until shortly after the Civil War that it became a military base. It was lent prominence by its proximity to nearby Chicago, but it became especially famous because of its eponymous first commander, Union general Philip H. Sheridan, whose pursuit of Gen. Robert E. Lee pushed the latter to surrender at Appomattox in April 1865, signaling the end of the Civil War. Since its beginnings, Fort Sheridan had been an enforcer of public order. When the civil fabric of Chicago was threatened by looting and other criminal activity following the Great Fire of 1871, General Sheridan and his troops exercised control over the chaotic city. Troops from the fort would also help put down the Pullman Strike in 1894, following which, wrote Col. John T. Rhett in his history of the fort, "the post had been practically deserted." All this is not to say that Fort Sheridan was a bleak backwater barrack, a hideout for riot police; it was as beautiful as the nurses claimed. Laid out on a rise flanked by ravines that fell to the shores of Lake Michigan below, Fort Sheridan benefited from a style consistently imposed by the same architecture firm that worked on the 632-acre site throughout the 1890s. By the time Donovan and Rags arrived at the fort in late 1918, the property boasted a wide range of structures—officers' quarters, commissary, veterinary hospital, stables, bachelor officers' quarters (with their own mess), ordnance storehouse, fire station—all situated roughly around the edges of an enormous oval-shaped parade ground. From the southern edge of the parade ground rose a 227-foot tower, which included a water tank, on either side of which were rows of barracks several stories high.[5]

There had been a base hospital on the Lake Michigan side of the property for some years. Colonel Rhett noted that there were four wards connected to the main building by covered porches, "erected for the sole purpose of meeting the normal expansion to be expected in a post of the size." Nobody then had any inkling just how much expansion would be needed, what Rhett terms a "$3,400,000 enterprise which was to grow on the spot." By the last year of the war, the numbers of wounded soldiers would be swelled by victims of the worldwide Spanish flu epidemic, necessitating the construction of many temporary wooden buildings to handle the overflow of patients and medical staff. Ultimately, forty-two new buildings were constructed on the parade ground, "used for wards, operating rooms, clinics, mess halls and the like," wrote Colonel Rhett. Incredibly unpatriotic as it sounds, there were complaints from the fort's neighbors, who disliked "the towering piles of yellow-white lumber, roofing, nails, sacks of cement, and other building materials" blocking their view of the parade ground's "verdant vastness," but eventually the piles of lumber rose into buildings. The first patients arrived on November 17, 1918, less than a week after the Armistice. Rohan specifically states that Donovan was brought to this complex, originally called Hospital No. 28, later known as Lovell General Hospital, and not to the hospital that predated it. Though it was dismantled two years after the end of the war, while it stood Lovell General was the nation's largest military hospital. Its official capacity was 4,800 beds; by the time the hospital closed, it had treated more than 60,000 sick and wounded. By late 1918, when Donovan arrived, the complex already had a trackless trolley system installed to ferry patients to treatments in clinics too distant for the disabled to walk or be carried to.[6]

Donovan would have been just one stretcher case among hundreds, but somehow, Rohan tells us, Rags's unknown rescuer from the hospital train got him safely through the depot crowds, then through the masses of stretchers till he found where Donovan sat, waiting to be transported into the hospital. That was where the soldier set Rags down. From that point on, Rags was on his own.

As at Brest, Rags tried to follow Donovan's stretcher, and as he had been on that day, he was rebuffed by medical staff who only saw a scruffy stray dog who kept getting in the way. But as at Brest, Rags had the good fortune to be recognized. As Rohan wrote, "While Rags was scouting around the hospital, getting a line on the chances of sneaking in, a large delegation of the post population was moving on the hospital for a look at Rags."[7] He was standing at the hospital door, through which Donovan's stretcher had just been carried, when a pair of medical officers who had heard his story put two and two together and clued in that he was trying to get in to see Donovan. They let Rags into the ward, where he visited with Donovan, now settled on a cot. When he saw that Donovan was being cared for, says Rohan, the terrier's wanderlust overcame him—as it would any dog in a new and different place—and he went out to investigate the lay of the land.

Aside from the parade ground, much of Fort Sheridan was characterized by uneven surfaces and ravines, which may have reminded Rags of rugged battlefield terrain in eastern France. Lake Michigan washed the east side of the fort's grounds, which fell both gradually and abruptly to the water's edge; this feature of the landscape seemed to interest him most. Rags was seen sitting there, gazing out over the water. Rohan does not speculate, but since Donovan was likely brought to Fort Sheridan sometime before Christmas, there was probably some snow on the ground or at least ice on the lake's surface.[8] Rags had certainly never seen this much water, frozen or otherwise, sequestered as he had been on his first and only Atlantic crossing. This must have presented a fascinating, perhaps disturbing sight to a dog who would have known snow in Paris but had likely only seen ice sheets no larger than frozen alleyway puddles.

Rohan says that when Rags returned to the hospital, nobody let him in. So he followed his nose to the mess hall kitchen, located almost directly behind the towered barrack block. There, as on so many of his days and nights in Montmartre and in battlefield mess halls, living off scraps proffered by kindly cooking staff, Rags was given something to eat. Thus fortified, he returned to the hospital, and this time somebody admitted him. He located Donovan's cot, crept under it, and slept for a while. Rohan says he was found later wandering through a ward and was chased out by a nurse. Rags returned to the mess kitchen and was fed again, and the staff made a bed for him there out of a pile of sacks, apparently thinking he would stay the night. Sometime after midnight, his barks were overheard by a passing officer. Through the opened door, Rags raced for the hospital entrance, but again couldn't get in. It was a terrible first day at Fort Sheridan for a tired and confused little dog.

Rohan speculates that later that night, unable to find any place in which to take shelter, Rags was drawn by voices—and possibly by aromas of food—in Fort Sheridan's fire station, just a few yards west of the mess hall. Luckily, the hours of the men there were not as regular as those of the rest of the base. Members of the station detail were having a last card game of the night when they heard a bark from just outside a door that had been left ajar. They let in a wet and very cold terrier. As Rags dried off in the warm interior, the men tried, as had so many before them, to teach him tricks. Rags was too tired to put his nose in the air and walk out, and in any case he had nowhere else to go. Rohan was told that when Rags entered the fire station, he shook his wet coat, crawled under the hose cart, and, after such a long and grueling day, slept.[9]

Until Rags actually had a home, which was not to be till more than a year in the future, this dark and protected spot among the coiled canvas hoses beneath the fire truck equipment was where he was safe. It is also likely under this hose cart that Rags spent his first and second Christmases in America, a firehouse mascot by default.

As it transpired, he would not have to wait outside the hospital doors again to see Donovan. Rohan says that after a couple of months, Rags had become a regular fixture at Fort Sheridan. He was allowed into the hospital by day, and while there he was permitted to lie alongside Donovan's cot. When he was put out at nightfall, Rags returned to the fire station, sure that the following day nobody would keep him away from his buddy. People noticed, as Rohan noted, that when Rags was with him, Donovan's condition seemed to improve; he seemed willing and able to fight to stay alive. Rags was being seen, however, as more than just Donovan's dog. Gradually everyone at the fort came to recognize and know Rags. Not only that, but the terrier's war record moved the men and women at Fort Sheridan to take pride in having on site a canine battle hero who was seen as belonging to everyone, from the wounded men recovering in the wards to the nurses who tended them and the officers who ran the fort.[10]

It was around this same time that Col. William N. Bispham, commandant and chief medical officer of Fort Sheridan from May 1919 until September 1920 (roughly the period during which Donovan was a patient), had a collar and tag made for Rags. It was as if Rags had become more than the post pet, as if he, like the men at the fort, needed to be formally recognized as a soldier who had put his life on the line, meriting proper acknowledgment and identification just as human soldiers did.

Rags's role as authentic symbol of American gallantry during the Great War was emphasized one evening when he was seen on his regular trot from the hospital to the mess kitchen doing something nobody at the fort had noticed before. "Rags happened along as the sunset gun boomed and the flag was coming down. Everybody was standing at the salute. The terrier proved that his memory of war days still was keen. He stopped in his tracks, stiffened, and lifted his right paw. Soldiers who noticed carried the news to the fire-house."[11] Probably nobody knew then that Rags had been taught this by Donovan. But it is just possible that someone—a nurse or medical officer, perhaps—told Donovan about it and heard that Rags had learned the salute from him. This only added to the growing store of Rags lore at the post to be shared with successive new arrivals.

In the middle of any grave illness, there is a point at which the sufferer feels almost content. It does not matter whether his disease worsens or improves, because he has reached a plateau of reconciliation and even comfort with his condition, which it appears might stabilize and never alter. Donovan's case was not one about which any medical professional could hold any naive hopes. His lungs were destroyed. This was 1920: lung transplants were over forty years in the future, and penicillin was not discovered till 1928. Having Rags beside his cot every day and evening had brought Donovan something approximating health, if a happy heart could override damaged tissue struggling to take in air. But if in his last weeks Donovan had reached a sort of bright zenith of mind over matter, after the high point came the descent. He could not fight anymore, sleeping almost all of the time. Rags was often seen standing at Donovan's cot, looking at his motionless figure.

As his relationship with Donovan became more the task of keeping vigil beside an unconscious body, Rags himself began to look as if he were suffering from a wasting disease, refusing to eat and appearing malnourished. Then, suddenly, Donovan was taken away to the critical ward in another part of the complex.

Because he didn't know where Donovan had been taken to, Rags assumed he was still in the same building. And once more, he was barred from the hospital. Rohan says that no sooner would Rags return to the fire station and lie down, exhausted, than he would run back again to the hospital, trying to get in. Just the speaking of Donovan's name, which naturally Rags recognized, would set him off in that direction. Rohan does say that Rags was finally able to get inside the hospital, because he was seen by nurses and orderlies in the ward where Donovan had been, walking between the rows of cots. As if dejected that he had not found Donovan, and preempting any efforts to put him out bodily, Rags waited beside the exit door and then returned to the fire station and his bed under the hose cart, where he lay in sleepless silence.

The story of Rags and Donovan might have ended right there, a precursor to a case of loyalty famous several years later when a dog named Hachiko began a nine-year wait at Shibuya Station in Tokyo for a master who never came home. But Col. William N. Bispham, who had given Rags his first collar and tag, had been told about Rags's hospital visit and saw that some official intervention was required.

Rohan describes Colonel Bispham, born in Culpeper, Virginia, in 1875 and schooled in Baltimore, Maryland, as a kind person. This is easy to believe, judging from a photograph taken around the time he was in charge of Fort Sheridan. Dr. Bispham's gentle eyes and smile glow through the sepia with a warm immediacy. Behind his kind expression was a truly good, honest, and fearless man who brooked no opposition to governing the fort, its patients, and its garrison with a compassionate hand. "I believe in men," he was quoted as saying in 1919, the year Donovan was a patient at Fort Sheridan. "When any of them has a complaint to make or a suggestion, he comes to me with it. I have tried to get the idea abroad that I wish them to. I am here to give them justice and have promised them that I would do so."[12] Colonel Bispham was so focused on restoring the mental and physical health of the roughly sixty thousand wounded soldiers who passed through Fort Sheridan that he risked letting down the side of discipline as it was commonly practiced and expected even from men who had returned from battle missing limbs or their sanity, "arguing that any unnecessary restraint would not further the recovery of these broken youngsters." Colonel Rhett wrote that "[Bispham] explained how the men had been relieved of duty in a field of violent action, forced to lie abed for months throughout cure and convalescence. . . . Naturally, they were impatient." When word of Bispham's tolerance of a wounded man's inability to salute a passing officer spread outside the boundaries of Fort Sheridan, he promised his superiors to straighten the men up, but he did it his way. Calling a mass meeting, Colonel Bispham explained the situation to all the men, asking that those who could conform to the rules do so as required. Such was the soldiers' respect for Bispham that "they resumed their old habits of smartness."[13] The student nurses at Fort Sheridan respected Bispham just as much, giving him all the credit for easing the jarring reassignments that occurred for them once the war had ended.[14]

Rohan says Colonel Bispham loved dogs. This he surely did, because after he heard from the hospital staff and the fire station detail about Rags's depression, he announced that he would take the terrier himself to the critical ward to see Donovan the next day. This was, needless to say, a very Bispham touch.

That night, however, Donovan died.

The following morning, Colonel Bispham arrived at the fire station to break the sad news. Appreciating the nuances of the situation and understanding that this had to be done right, one of the station detail, a young westerner who had been raised with dogs, told the colonel he knew how to make Rags understand what had happened to his guardian. The young man picked Rags up and walked with Colonel Bispham to the critical ward. The soldier sat Rags on Donovan's empty cot, its sheets still unchanged. Taking Rags's grief as seriously as he would that of a human soldier, the fireman explained that Donovan had gone away, that that was how it was, and that Rags had to accept it.

Anyone who knows dogs is aware of the stages of their grieving. Their favorite person leaves for only a few days, but for the dog it is forever. There is waiting and pining at doors and windows and jumping to investigate every remotely familiar sound, which could just be the longed-for person returning home. Then the change comes, almost imperceptibly, and can be just as sad, in its way, as the depression, because the dog seems gallantly determined to face loss by adopting new loves, new faces to watch and footsteps to listen for. Behind it all, the longing for the original person is still there, and if that person does return, the dog's joy is uncontainable. Rags was no exception to this pattern, but as with every challenge in his life, he quickly adapted. Rohan was told that on being placed on the bed, Rags "sniffed, stretched himself, his forepaws extended and nose buried between them, and lay motionless for more than a minute." He then hopped to the floor and headed for the ward's exit.[15]

As the young soldier's remedy for Rags proves, soldiers at Fort Sheridan understood that animals love and miss people as much as people do.

Over the following days, Rags was carefully watched, his behavior monitored and his pain ameliorated as best anyone could guess how, just as the men might keep an eye out for depression in a shell-shocked soldier returned from war. Rags was lucky in having these men around him to ease his pain, and he was lucky in that he was young. Rags spent a week displaying the same behavior he'd shown during Donovan's last days, lying quietly under the hose cart, completely uninterested in food.

Hunger and, perhaps, a dog's sense of the appropriate period for mourning brought Rags back to his meals and, in turn, to the places he loved to visit—the stables where the horses were, the officers' club, and, of course, the mess halls. But there was one place he never returned to again—the hospital where Donovan had died.

7

Family

On May 16, 1903, almost seventeen years before Rags arrived in Illinois and thirteen years before his birth, a young American couple, Lt. Raymond Waite Hardenbergh and Miss Helen Wolcott Stewart Johnson, whose lives were to be intimately entwined with his, were married in a lavish Chicago church ceremony.[1]

Both Raymond and Helen came from old American stock, he from wealthy slave-owning Dutch patroons from New York State, she from *Mayflower* passengers and New England pioneers. And both loved animals of all kinds, perhaps their deepest shared bond of all.[2]

After the wedding, Raymond and Helen had a short honeymoon in California, then sailed westward to Raymond's assignment in the Philippines. Not much is known about Raymond's military career, but there are some tantalizing clues. The couple's grandson Raymond G. H. Seitz, former U.S. ambassador to the United Kingdom, owns a saber forged in Toledo, Spain, and engraved with the Spanish royal arms but is unsure whether Raymond captured the sword in the Spanish-American War or purchased it as a curio in Cuba or the Philippines. There is a newspaper photograph of Raymond with other members of his company, sitting in the former palace of rebel leader and first president of the Philippines, Emilio Aguinaldo. "Lieutenant Hardenbergh seems quite satisfied with his lot," states the article.[3] Raymond Seitz writes that much of Lieutenant Hardenbergh's military history is a blur because, as with the records of so many American soldiers who served in World War I and earlier conflicts, his war documents went up in smoke in the 1973 fire at the National Personnel Records Center in St. Louis. Raymond Hardenbergh's 1949 obituary is the best source for his record of service, from the Spanish-American War, through the Philippine insurrection, in which many of the men in Rags's circle took part, down to World War I and World War II. In 1918, the same year Rags entered the theater of war, Raymond sailed to France. He served as brigade adjutant with the Eightieth Division and then on the staff of General Pershing. Precise details are lacking, but even so, writes Ambassador Seitz, while Raymond was on Pershing's staff, he "might have heard about Rags." Ambassador Seitz doesn't fail to recognize one salient fact: thanks to Rags's fame, Raymond Hardenbergh's military career is certainly more traceable than it would have been otherwise.[4]

Just when in 1920 the Hardenberghs and their young daughters, Helen (fifteen) and Susan (seven), arrived at Fort Sheridan is not known—Hardenbergh was accepted as major on September 24, 1920, so it may have been around then. There may be another clue in an interview with Helen Hardenbergh published in June 1926. "Rags knew us at the hospital [at Fort Sheridan]," Helen explained. "He had formed the habit of dropping in for meals, so he just naturally attached himself to us after Sergeant Donovan died." Helen was aware that Donovan's "great wish was that somebody would take care of his pal." It's clear from this that the Hardenberghs arrived at the fort shortly before Donovan's death rather than after, which sounds as if Donovan could have been alive well into 1920.[5]

By the time the Hardenberghs had arrived at Fort Sheridan, Rags was an indelible part of the post's daily life. Since Donovan's passing, Rags had met many other patients, soldiers, mess cooks, officers, and visitors at Fort Sheridan. He would have been aware of the commotion around a terrorism crisis in February 1919, when suitcases containing time bombs were discovered near the hospital, an act attributed, as Colonel Rhett surmised, to "foreign agitators or stubborn sympathizers of the defeated Central Powers." The press was not encouraged to follow this up lest the publicity earn the fort more bomb attempts or copycats. Rags was also present at the fort when Colonel Bispham dealt with threats of another kind, these from the Chicago Chamber of Commerce. Upon hearing rumors that the last members of the original garrison had departed the post in May, the worthies of the chamber protested that the property should be returned to the city, since the original grant stipulated this in the event the land was no longer used as a garrison. Colonel Bispham, with characteristic humor, pointed out that he still had in his command 1,100 men and 150 officers. "Does that look as if the Fort were being abandoned?" he asked. Furthermore, he noted that if "North Shore people" were so upset that the property was off bounds to their "social and welfare activities," as they claimed, they could rest assured. "The hospital was a worthy object for their benefactions . . . and its area hungry for entertainment and their social efforts."[6]

Perhaps the best proof that Fort Sheridan was nowhere close to being abandoned was that Rags was able to live off the land there, as it were, very well indeed. Spending his nights at the fire station, he had his meals not only at the nearby mess but in a variety of households all over the fort. "Company messes, officers' club, the kitchens of the married officers were all on his list," wrote Rohan. One of these married officers' kitchens was eventually that of Raymond and Helen Hardenbergh. Helen employed a cook, so it was likely she rather than a family member who fed Rags on his first visit to the house. Having dined, he moved on, according to his usual method. "They saw no more of him, for a time," noted Rohan. But then Rags discovered something that to him, clearly, was more valuable even than food. Rags fell in love with Raymond Hardenbergh's daughters.[7]

Helen and Sue Hardenbergh had to commute to Winnetka each day to attend school, a trip of a little over a dozen miles by rail, which started at the Fort Sheridan fire station. There, the girls made a habit of leaving the bicycles they rode from their parents' quarters, then picking them up again on their return in the afternoon. One afternoon on their return from school, they were confronted by Rags, who made bold to press his suit on the girls without a prior introduction. Rohan says the girls were afraid of the twenty-five-pound monster and ran home to tell their father.[8]

According to Rohan, Raymond Hardenbergh had been doing a fair amount of research on Fort Sheridan's mascot. Rohan asserts that though the girls' father extolled Rags's bravery in battle, this did little to convince them to accept his friendship; they continued to have nothing to do with him. But Rags pursued the children, waiting for them beside their bikes after school and chasing them down the road, or ambushing them from stands of weeds as they sped away. Then Rags insinuated himself into the Hardenbergh kitchen just when Sue came in for her after-school snack. "The fear the child felt when she met the terrier at the fire-station vanished," Rohan says, as both girl and dog munched on their food. When Sue told Rags that he was "a nice doggie," the terrier stood happily, "tail vibrating like a big, fuzzy tuning fork. . . . He sat up and lifted his paws, a gesture he seldom made."[9]

Hardenbergh family photographs tell the truest story. Each shows, in the course of the next sixteen years, just how loved and integral a member of the family Rags was, whether sprawling on parade-ground grass with girlfriends of Sue and Helen, sitting in Sue's lap on her father's front porch or on a sled in snow, or nestling against Major Hardenbergh. From this point on, both Sue and Helen were infatuated with Rags and began to make concerted efforts to convince their father that the terrier should come into their house to live (Mrs. Hardenbergh doesn't seem to have needed convincing). While not averse to the idea, Raymond knew there was a fair amount of protocol to contend with. He explained to his daughters that while Rags was a wonderful, friendly companion, he was not a stray but belonged to the post as a whole—he was "a member of the army, as it were," wrote Rohan, "and . . . no individual could lay any claim to him."[10] But the girls' pleading had the desired effect. Acknowledging that it would take nothing away from Rags's independence and others' claims on him to give him a place of lodging, Raymond made him a bed in a corner using a folded blanket, and it was there, after some initial puzzlement, that Rags took up his abode in the Hardenberghs' home. This simple bed in a small officer's bungalow at Fort Sheridan was the first time in years, and perhaps the first time ever, that the dog of war rescued from a Montmartre gutter had a real home, in every sense of the word, one in which he could live without fear of eviction.

Thanks to this proximity to his new family, we learn quite a bit about the terrier that we might otherwise not have known. Several years after Rags's adoption, Helen Johnson Hardenbergh provided a list of all his personality traits, much as one would describe an eccentric but beloved member of the family:

"He has many funny customs. He likes soldiers, but is suspicious of civilians. . . . He is very fond of sweets and is always going down to the canteen, where the soldiers give him tidbits. And he enjoys the movies, too. Whenever there is a show he is usually under some soldier's chair.

"Rags dislikes a sudden noise. I guess he is shell-shocked. When the time comes for the retreat gun to go off he begins scratching at the front door. He wants to get in and hide under the sofa. And he hates the noise of firecrackers. But he is as faithful as they make them. Whenever I am away he sleeps under my little daughter's [Sue's] bed."[11]

Rags and the Hardenbergh girls were a perfect match. They loved to romp and run, and so did he. They knew without being told that Rags disliked efforts to teach him tricks, and so they never bothered him in this way. Rags maintained his many casual friendships in virtually every household and barrack at Fort Sheridan, though breakfast, dinner and bed were provided at the Hardenberghs'. There remained the matter of where he was to get his lunch, along with the sweets he couldn't live without. Yet as integral a presence as the dog was in the Fort Sheridan community, it was dawning on everyone who knew him that Rags was somehow no longer theirs. Still, this was not an official status, as was clarified when Raymond received orders to proceed to his next posting: Fort Benning in southwest Georgia.

Rohan writes that when Raymond tried to reason with Helen and Sue and explain that Rags would have to remain at Fort Sheridan, "the children couldn't see it that way at all. They 'went politician,' as the saying is, and canvassed all of the influential persons on the post, not overlooking the commandant [Colonel Bispham]." Their argument? It was simple, and it couldn't be denied: before the Hardenberghs had arrived at Fort Sheridan, Rags was homeless. He had had the fire station to stay in, the hose cart to sleep under, tidbits in the mess, many hands to pat him. But he had not had a home until the Hardenberghs made one for him. As the girls argued, "It wasn't fair to make him homeless again."[12]

A vote—or the semblance of one—was taken by all the men, according with Colonel Bispham's respect for the democratic process. The consensus that issued from the referendum was that "the children were declared trustees of Rags in so far as the post council had authority to declare it."[13]

It may have been shortly after this that Major Hardenbergh had a new collar made for Rags. This one was a lot like his Fort Sheridan collar, a basic band of thick black leather studded with rows of decorative metal buttons. But on this collar was riveted an engraved metal tag and a new identity that would serve as a calling card among aging veterans who may have never thought they would reunite with the little dog from the battlefields of France. Along with Rags's name and that of Major Hardenbergh were placed emblems of the terrier's battlefield career, chevrons marking his war service and his wounds suffered in battle. Rags wore this identity tag and the fame that came with it for the next sixteen years.

8

Governors Island

Whether Rags ever ventured to the Gare du Nord in Paris, not far from his haunt in Montmartre, or was nearby when the station came close to being hit by a German shell in 1917, we will never know. But it was at that other French train station, the Gare de Brest, where he was almost parted from Sergeant Donovan. And the American stations he'd experienced were hardly mileposts of joy during his long, cramped journeys under cots and in handbags at Hoboken and Fort Sheridan. Still, Manhattan's palatial Grand Central Station in 1925 would have been a different experience altogether. It was probably as confusing to the terrier as Rohan writes, that Rags "kept on the jump to avoid being stepped on, even though the major [Hardenbergh] guided him with a leash."[1] Yet Grand Central was more than a train station for the dog and his human family. It was truly the portal to a life neither Rags nor the Hardenberghs could ever have imagined.

Like all military families, the Hardenberghs had moved often. But the Fort Sheridan living quarters, which to them were just a way station en route to other military housing somewhere else, had likely been the only home Rags had ever known. Their bungalow was above all else the place in which he had found reliable shelter after three years of shifting for himself on the streets of Paris, on the battlefields of eastern France, and in the fort. So of course, as it does for any pet when its guardians move, the Hardenberghs' packing made Rags all the more nervous. Rohan says the terrier stayed as close to Sue and Helen as he could, watching their every action as if to be prepared to leave the house when they did, as if to make sure he was not left behind.

The family's journey, which took them southwest to Fort Benning, in Chattahoochee County, Georgia, held many unknowns for all of them, but especially for Rags. This was not the kind of train trip he had been accustomed to make, whether through France or across the United States. In those days, under Donovan's cot or in an officer's handbag, Rags had always been protected en route somewhere by the presence of soldiers. For the trip to Georgia, a journey of over eight hundred miles, Rags had to travel alone in the baggage car among the trunks and suitcases. At first, says Rohan, Rags had panicked, as if fearing he was being sent away from his family. Noticing this, every time the train stopped the Hardenbergh girls ran back to see him. This put Rags at ease, as if riding in the baggage car was merely another form of the clandestine travel arrangements he had experienced on the hospital ship and during his train ride from Hoboken to Fort Sheridan. All this attention moved the chief baggage-man to make enquiries of the family, from whom he learned that his car contained a real war hero. When the chief baggage-man saluted him, Rags offered what was for him a rare return salute to a man not wearing military uniform. On the strength of this alone, Rags received the royal treatment the rest of the way to Georgia.[2]

After all the upheaval of packing and transport, the Hardenberghs' next posting must have seemed eerily quiet. This was a result not so much of its remote location but because, like many army posts during the 1920s, Fort Benning (given that name in 1922) was virtually cut off from most government funding and attention and at one point was almost shut down for good. Just a few years earlier, during the war, it had been a far busier place. As the location of the United States Army Infantry School and a noisy training ground for artillery and gunners, Fort Benning helped mold some future five-star generals (among them George C. Marshall and George S. Patton). But the base wasn't really to come alive again until the 1930s, when federal works projects arising across the bankrupt nation helped raise several prominent structures at the camp and establish its permanence on the landscape.[3]

At the time of the Hardenbergh family's arrival, Fort Benning was still pretty basic. While the commandant's headquarters were located in the pillared plantation house that had come with the land, the officers' quarters were not quite so splendid, and the little shacks where the noncommissioned officers lived looked like sharecroppers' dwellings. The Hardenberghs, preoccupied with getting their lives in order and possibly not thinking about the fact that there were snakes and other predators in Georgia that Rags would never have encountered in France or Illinois, allowed the terrier plenty of leeway to explore the property's expanse of red clay soil, gravel, and straight-backed pines. While doing so, Rags encountered a more familiar threat than rattlers.

At what point Rags first met the camp's police dog Rohan does not say, but from the start the bigger dog simply did not care for this small and shaggy interloper. Whenever Rags was within sight or smell of him, the police dog snapped, growled, and lunged in his direction. The dog was kept tied up when not out on patrol with his handler, which meant he was tethered most of the time. A case hardly has to be made for the stress, deprivation of socialization, and inability to move freely suffered by a dog kept constantly on tether. A chained dog, seeing another one that was free to go where it wanted, would naturally be frustrated, so much so that, if it got free, its aggression would know no restraint.

When Rags was crossing an open area one day, the police dog broke loose and lunged for him. "He doesn't go around looking for a fight," Rags's guardian Helen Hardenbergh once told a reporter, "but I've never seen him try to avoid one."[4] Members of the garrison received the same impression. As they ran toward where the large dog was about to leap on the small one, they were baffled that Rags did not flee but stood where he was. Rohan says Rags "met the attack without flinching"; he even tried to climb on the larger dog's back, knowing from experience of past street battles that the spine was the weak point, even in a dog several times his size. Amid the yelping and snarling and flying fur, "military police pounded the police dog with their clubs," says Rohan; "officers and soldiers kicked one another's shins in an effort to boot Rags's assailant into retreat." Rags, with a determination judged well nigh suicidal, would not let go of the police dog's nose. Water had to be thrown over the dogs twice before they were separated, and then Major Hardenbergh had to use all his strength at the other end of Rags's leash to keep the little terrier from leaping on the police dog again. Rags's insane but glorious bravery earned him many admirers among the dog-loving men of Fort Benning, and as a result his presence at the garrison was more prized than before, though now the men were more careful to watch out for his safety. Which is why the entire population of Fort Benning turned out in force when, shortly after this fight, Rags disappeared.[5]

Rags's occasional abscondings were nothing new and didn't especially worry the Hardenberghs or anyone else who knew him. The fort, which at the time encompassed more than one hundred thousand acres, was surrounded by pine woods and scrub, and along one side ran the Chattahoochee River. It was perfect territory for an extended Rags expedition, though also the perfect place for a dog unfamiliar with the property to get lost.

Rags's absence on the first day was no cause for alarm, says Rohan. When he didn't appear the next, a general search was ordered.

Given the terrain, there was no lack of possible places where the dog could be, but nobody could find him in any of them. Then Major Hardenbergh, having a hunch that Rags might be closer to home, backtracked from the camp's grounds to his family's living quarters. And it was there, in the coal-bin under the house, that he found Rags, "a bloody, broken little bundle," says Rohan, "more dead than alive." How Rags had got there in his condition and how long he had been there were anybody's guess. The Hardenberghs told Rohan it was as if every bone in his body had been fractured.[6]

The Fort Benning veterinarian was called to the house to render his verdict. It was grim: Rags had been struck by a car. In light of his early life spent in congested Paris, Rags's terror of automobiles seems peculiar, but he had obviously had close calls with them before. It is known that anytime he found himself in heavy traffic, as Rohan reports, Rags would freeze. On later excursions into Manhattan, the terrier who hated being picked up under any circumstances would stand stock still on the sidewalk until someone arrived to carry him safely across a busy street.

Perhaps while he was sniffing along some dirt road around the post's perimeter, Rags became transfixed by an oncoming car and unable to move out of the way until it was too late. If he didn't hear or see the car, with a blind eye and deaf ear on his right side, his creaky war-wounded body might not have been able to get out of the way in time. (On a future occasion, he would be saved by a quick-thinking soldier from just this kind of near-accident.)

The injured dog was transferred to a blanket and brought into the house, where he was placed on the floor beside the living room fire-place. Rags remained there for days. He lifted his head occasionally to drink water but ate nothing.[7] And for the time and place, this for most animal owners was considered the best one could do. A century into the future, Rags would have had the benefit of X-rays to determine the full extent of his injuries, along with intravenous fluids and painkillers to make him comfortable. If there were broken bones, they would be set and wrapped, and there would be frequent checkups. But in the mid-1920s, a dog as grievously injured as Rags was would have ordinarily been euthanized, and not necessarily in a way that would be considered humane today—those were the days when an injured or mortally ill horse or a dog was taken behind the barn and shot. Though there was a growing awareness that animals experienced pain and deserved the same treatment for it as a human being, advanced care for an injured domestic animal was not yet in place. The American Society for the Prevention of Cruelty to Animals (ASPCA), founded in 1866, came as close as the American nineteenth-century world could to arguing for the right to a pain-free life for animals, especially those compelled to serve human purposes.[8] Though the American Veterinary Medical Association was founded three years before the ASPCA, the vets of Rags's time were still mostly employed to look after larger animals. These were mainly draft horses or livestock, with care for the latter more to ensure sanitary milk and beef for human consumption than to look after the animals' physical and emotional welfare.

So as incredible as it sounds, considering the injuries Rags was alleged to have suffered, besides love and a comfortable place to lie and water when he wanted it, not much else was done for the broken and bloodied terrier. There is no evidence he had any intention of giv-ing up this battle, any more than he had with any other. Rohan tells us that throughout his recovery, Rags never made a sound; only when Sue or Helen visited with him would he risk the supreme effort of trying to wag his tail while still prone on the floor. That he was not summarily put down says as much about how much he meant to his adoptive family as it does about how bravely he faced his grave injuries.

In the end, Rags proved to have more lives than the proverbial cat. He did recover and in fact was strong and, as Rohan puts it, even frisky enough to take pleasure in the prospect of another long journey, which came almost overnight. Soon after the Hardenberghs arrived in Georgia, Major Hardenbergh was posted to Camp Knox in Kentucky, near Louisville, then reassigned for the summer to the training camp at Plattsburgh, New York, on the banks of Lake Champlain, another large body of water for Rags to fish in and stare at with distant fascination.

Other than its normal school (later a state university of New York) and its training camp, Plattsburg, as it was then spelled, didn't have much to pin it to the map. But as with other small towns, where there is a civilian college and a military presence, both contributed to an explosive alchemy of political unrest and protest that was at odds with Plattsburg's placid atmosphere.

The timing was just right for such combustion. Major Hardenbergh's arrival came toward the end of the so-called Red Scare of 1919-24. During these years, membership in the Communist Party of America could bring as much trouble to a card-carrying member as it would a quarter century later in the McCarthy witch-hunt years of the 1950s. No longer having to operate underground, party members were free to be more visible, which is why a small group of them gathered one day in a Plattsburg park, lecturing bystanders on their civil duties. One of these, shouted the man standing on a soap-box, was the right to refuse to participate in war, that well-oiled machine that enriched capitalists as it ground up soldiers like so much mulch. Rohan says that Rags, on one of his jaunts through town, came to a stop near the crowd, members of which were either jeering at or agreeing with the speaker.

Rohan was obviously no lover of Communists, using them in *Rags* as convenient stereotypes for purposes of amusement. Because of this, the scene Rohan describes could well be invented, but it was historically possible, as is the scene that happened next. Apparently it wasn't enough for Rags to have sunk his teeth into the boots of Kaiser Bill's troops in the battlefields of France. When pointed at by the soap-box Communist as an example of a "yellow dog"—parlance for the type of selfish bourgeois coward he was deriding—Rags barked and snarled at the man. In response, one of the speaker's cohorts tried to kick Rags. This was a big mistake. Some of the Plattsburg training camp soldiers, who would have agreed with the old soldier who told Helen Hardenbergh, "Rags may be yaller on the outside but he ain't inside," were present to witness this attempt to hurt their mascot.[9]

A fight ensued between Communists and trainees, during which Rags was said to have gone airborne to grab a blackjack just as a Communist was about to land it on the head of a soldier. "A slash of his teeth forced the blackjack from the man's hand," says Rohan, as if sketching an action scene for a film script. Further underscoring the cinematic flavor of events, Rohan has everyone taken to the police station, Rags trotting along behind the paddy wagon. (One can almost envision the final shot focusing in on Rags's "gaily carried tail.") At the station, Rohan claims Rags was successfully put forward as principal witness to identify which of the Communists was the primary troublemaker, though how he did this he doesn't say.

This scene, even if partly or wholly imaginary, tells a lot about what Rags, like Sergeant Stubby and a host of other mascots, had come to symbolize to members of the military. For Jimmy Donovan, Rags was at first a battlefield buddy and later an equal partner in the trenches without whom Donovan could not have done his job as soldier or survived mentally and emotionally—the equivalent of a modern therapy dog. For Major Hardenbergh and his family, Rags was a lovable companion who needed a home and who happened to have a glowing war record, of which all were justifiably proud and which their descendants venerate to this day. For others, Rags was and is a symbol of the First Division at its finest, a source of pride that grew in luster with each of his real or imagined acts of bravery. And for the men in Plattsburg—and likely for many other soldiers who admired him—Rags's military career was joined to a form of anthropomorphism, as if it were a given that Rags, were he human, would share their own beliefs, including the anti-Communist feeling of many in the military.

More significantly, though, in view of what was to happen next, is how Rags came to be seen during this time in comparison with other dogs. Rohan writes that the trainees took Rags's history very seriously, again projecting their own inexperience against his war record, matching their enthusiasm for battle glory with what was presumed to be his. "When their friend or relatives turned up [at Plattsburg] with pedigreed dogs," Rohan says, "the boys would point to Rags and challenge the show dogs to match his record."[10]

This pride in Rags's achievements, unlike the regimental rivalries over which unit he preferred, remained within the precincts of military bases. Yet it would shortly take on a life of its own outside the martial sphere of army forts and into the rarefied setting of dog shows, those phenomena that first captivated democratic America's wider attention in the first decades of the twentieth century. The only blood that counted at these thoroughbred events was unspilled and blue—that is, until a red-blooded military hero and his military sponsors arrived to shake things up.

Shaped roughly like one of Rags's favorite things, a freshly scooped ice cream cone, Governors Island lies an eight-hundred-yard ferry sail off the southernmost tip of Manhattan.

Known to precolonial Native Americans as Nut Island after the many nut-bearing trees then covering the land, the island was first put to use for military purposes by the Dutch in 1633. The name by which it was known when Rags and the Hardenberghs lived there (ca. 1924–29) was bestowed in the late eighteenth century when the island was the exclusive resort of the prerevolutionary royal governors of New York. Since that period, the island continued to serve as the first line of defense for New York Harbor and even as a military prison during the Civil War. Fort Jay was the island's base, named in honor of United States founding father John Jay, and it was headquarters for the Sixteenth Infantry, a circumstance that was to lead to a reunion between Rags and the only living soldier who had known him before he joined the First Division.

Posted to the Inspector General's Office, Second Corps HQ, at Fort Jay, Major Hardenbergh and his family settled into a two-story married officer's residence with ornate white iron porch railings.[11] At first, so far as most of the men posted to Fort Jay were concerned, Rags was just another dog brought in by an officer they barely knew. Indeed, Governors Island could easily have been nicknamed "Dog Island." Besides Rags, there were collies, a bulldog, a Highland terrier, and a fierce chow, to name a few.[12] Many of the current crop of servicemen were too young to have fought in the war, let alone to have known Rags. Others, the survivors of the campaigns of 1917–18, "a leaven of old-timers," as Rohan puts it, were for the most part noncommissioned officers "whose duties kept them to their offices."[13] Any who may have idly glanced out a window at the scruffy little terrier shuffling his way across the green space may have gone back to his paperwork without another thought. But Rags knew who they were and took his explorations indoors. That's when the old-timers realized they had a hero in their midst, one who all had assumed had been killed years earlier in France.

Rohan doesn't state which of these old-timers made the identification first. As Rags paid more visits to offices, kitchens, and messes, however, it dawned on some of the men that the fuzzy dog with a blind eye, a cough, and a limp looked a lot like the terrier they had fought beside at Saint-Mihiel or the Argonne in 1918. Somebody then noticed that the dog had a name tag on his collar that seemed to spell out his history pretty conclusively. The men went to Major Hardenbergh for confirmation. Not only did he affirm that this was *the* First Division Rags, but he told them the rest of his and Donovan's postwar story, ensuring the legend's dissemination throughout the base. "Rags became, so far as the old-timers were concerned, the living symbol of the division's valor," wrote Rohan. Moreover, the younger soldiers now bent an ear to his story; they, too, would spread it through their own ranks.[14]

Having added to his human fan club, Rags quietly enlisted the Fort Jay collies, a pair belonging to an officer's wife. These were white-and-golden beauties, immaculately groomed, often decorated with ribbons by their proud guardian. Perhaps it was Rags's very visible freedom—freedom to go where he wished, freedom to do without baths or brushings or bows—that attracted these show dogs. His generosity, which Rags was to demonstrate to most dogs as to most people, was certainly a draw: he began to save any bones left over from what he was given by the Hardenberghs and by the Fort Jay cook and then give them to his friends the collies.[15] Perhaps he knew he needed as many allies as he could get, because, as with the police dog at Fort Benning, Rags had a deadly enemy at Fort Jay.

"Those who have no more sense than to own a vicious dog—few dogs are really vicious—can't be expected to have sense enough to keep them always tied up," wrote Rohan. On Governors Island there was a chow

chow, kept continually tied in its yard, that disliked Rags on sight. The lion dogs of imperial China, chows have a marked tendency to protect their territory and their owners with fierce alacrity, and their hunting instinct can be strong. Having yanked at its chain one time too many, the chow finally broke free, got out of its yard, and headed for Rags. As at Fort Benning, seeing what was about to happen, all available men rushed to Rags's defense. And again, as the artillery trainees had found, their efforts were to no avail, thanks to Rags's unwillingness to back off from his much larger opponent, who in this case was covered with such thick fur that there was no way Rags's smaller mouth and teeth could gain any purchase. The chow was getting the best of Rags, and a soldier was about to swing a billy-club at it when "a couple of white-and-gold thunderbolts almost knocked him over." Rags's collies leaped on the chow with such ferocity that it fought free and ran off. They refused to give chase, Rohan says, preferring to sit alongside Rags and lick his war-wounded ear where the chow had torn it.[16]

Rags's bravery in this second of his unprovoked dog fights on a military base and his thrilling willingness to face an unequal battle did nothing to lower his status in the eyes of the men of Governors Island. In fact, it rather swelled the heads of H Company, Sixteenth Infantry, in particular, to such a degree that they insisted that Rags was actually a member of their outfit by deliberate choice. As evidence, H Company pointed to the fact that Rags visited their mess almost every day while rarely poking his nose into the other units' messes.[17] Nobody seemed to reason that this might be due to H Company's superior and/or generous mess chef rather than to a special connection to the men. That was not to come until a few years later, and through one of them in particular.

Rags had helped the Sixteenth hold Hill 272 in the Argonne, but his affections were more liberally shared, as he was to prove.

Not long after the fight with the chow, Rags was seen to pay great attention to some soldiers who arrived at Governors Island each day via a ferry across Buttermilk Channel.

"These soldiers and officers wore the shoulder shield of the First Division," says Rohan, "but the regimental insignia of the Eighteenth Infantry."[18] They were stationed at Fort Hamilton, Brooklyn, where

First Division headquarters was located; they only came over to the island because that was where Gen. Hugh A. Drum (another friend of Rags's from France), area commander for Second Corps, had his offices.

Rags had a fascination with water—not to bathe in, of course, but to look at, fish in, and now travel over, which he did one evening with amazing laissez-faire. He jumped into the launch just as the Hamilton men were returning to Brooklyn, and when a Fort Jay sergeant objected, pointing out that the Hardenbergh girls would be heartbroken should Rags not appear all night (obviously having heard of the Fort Benning car collision), a senior officer promised to telephone Major Hardenbergh with Rags's whereabouts. If Rags wished to pay a call on First Division HQ, pay a call he must.

"In such fashion, Rags made his first visit to Fort Hamilton," wrote Rohan. "There were men in the Eighteenth infantry who had known him in France; more than that, there were men in the headquarters who had known Donovan." The fact that Rags had "chosen" to visit First Division HQ allowed the men to conclude that, far from being partial to the Sixteenth Infantry, it was the Eighteenth that actually captured the terrier's heart—another mistaken assumption, as it happened.[19]

Young Sue Hardenbergh certainly knew better. When told that Rags planned to spend a second day at Fort Hamilton, Sue refused to believe that he did so because he preferred the Eighteenth Infantry over the Sixteenth. It was the overweening vanity of the H Company soldiers that had brought this jaunt about, she concluded. "He's just gone away to show them," insisted Sue. "Now maybe they'll stop it." Sue was right. After visiting everyone—the human, canine, and feline populations of Fort Hamilton—and tasting all the cooking offered to him, Rags was found waiting for the launch the morning of his third day at Fort Hamilton. When he reached Governors Island he hurried up to the Hardenbergh girls—as if, Rohan wrote, to say to them, "Well, I'm back, and I hope you're glad to see me." They were. But while Rags did seem glad to be back in their care, he had received more than a taste of Fort Hamilton's mess kitchen menus on this adventure. "Rags's trip to Hamilton apparently gave him a zest for voyaging," wrote Rohan.[20]

When the ferry docked as usual at Governors Island one morning not long after Rags's return from Brooklyn, the terrier casually stepped aboard for the short sail to lower Manhattan. He was allowed to remain onboard by an officer who, again, overrode the objections of the crew (leading one to conclude that these incidents were not so much for Rags's benefit as they were to score points between ranks as well as regiments).

Rohan writes that after the mail carrier reached State Street, he heard barking just behind him. He turned to find Rags waiting on the far curb. The carrier recognized him and went back across, returning with Rags under his arm. Thus it was at the side of a mailman, alleged foe of dogs, that Rags first entered the square-jawed, red-brick, and red-granite Army Building at 39 Whitehall Street. Rohan reports that everyone was glad to see Rags, his story having spread far, though they were puzzled as to why or how he had managed to get there. Before taking him back to Governors Island, a recruiting sergeant carried Rags upstairs to the office of Army Information Service (a branch of the military with which Rohan worked during the Great War and during World War II as well). The sergeant had known both Donovan and Rags in France, and to the officer seated at the desk he gladly gave a full introduction, including everything he remembered about Donovan and the terrier. Impressed by the story, the officer saluted Rags and was charmed and moved when Rags lifted his paw alongside his face in response—he had not forgotten Donovan's lessons in proper military decorum. Eager to capture Rags's history, the officer asked the sergeant to recount it again as he wrote it down. Finishing, the officer then turned to the terrier and said, "Rags, you are elected to become famous here and now." These words were not lightly spoken; the AIS was to do as much as the New York press to make Rags a household name.[21]

Somebody had the idea of taking a photograph of Rags. All went well until, smelling the powder used in the photographer's flash gun, Rags reacted. He "hopped off the desk and flattened himself on the floor," wrote Rohan, "just as he had learned to do when he heard the rattle of shell coming his way in the old war days."[22]

After getting shots of Rags and of each other with him, the men made sure the terrier was escorted back to the ferry in the company of an officer who knew enough only to carry Rags across the street and put him down again so he could regain his dignity before boarding the vessel.

Once on the ferry, as if to the rank promoted, Sergeant Rags hopped straight up to the officers' deck without further ado. Soldiers were smiling on both the dock and the boat. Rags just stood in the sea breeze, nose pointed toward home.

9

Fame

Despite a formal order from Governors Island forbidding Rags to be allowed to board the New York ferry, the terrier found other means and occasions for travel.

For instance, when a mine-planter from Fort Hancock at Sandy Hook, New Jersey, put in at Governors Island, Rags jumped at the chance to go aboard and head south, where he delighted the First Engineers with a surprise appearance.

At Fort Hancock, reported Rohan, Rags "ran into a regular old-home party. On all sides were men he had run across in the old days. . . . Rags was no legend to them; he was as closely linked to their lives as the battle scars on their bodies."[1]

Rags was given a party at the fort during which he received copious treats and attention. A comfortable bed was made up for him to spend the night, but he did not sleep. In the wee hours, men who were on duty reported seeing him wandering all over the post, from one side of the peninsula to the other. Only at dawn did he rest (which necessitated his staying another day). No one could figure out what his night ramble had been about, and for Rags to not take advantage of a comfortable place to sleep was unusual. Was it just his peculiar fascination with large bodies of water? Or had all the familiar faces of Fort Hancock sent him in search of Donovan's?

On the day of his return to Governors Island, after a command demanding his restoration, Rags's ferry reached the dock just after a group of reporters had ferried over to the island to meet him. They had to sail away empty handed. "The army information officer had told the world about the terrier," says Rohan. The picture of Rags sitting on the desk in the Army Building at 39 Whitehall, along with his story, had made it into the papers.[2] There was no turning back now: the dog, so to speak, was out of the bag. From this time on, as Rohan aptly describes, Rags began to pay "the price of prominence."

Part of that price involved Rags having to endure the presence of the press. They raised his hackles just by coming up the walkway. Yet more and more of these intrepid newsmen made the short sail over to Governors Island to interview Rags—or, rather, to interview his family, because the famous terrier always made himself scarce when they arrived. When one reporter stopped at the Hardenbergh residence, he had to content himself with the gracious conversation of Helen Hardenbergh. Rags remained upstairs until the interview was almost concluded, only edging down the steps and into the foyer when Helen spoke his name and reached out a hand to stroke his head.

This interview is, incidentally, one of the earliest extant instances in which Rags is described in photographic detail: he was "a long, yellow-haired mut[t] with one ear which falls over his blind eye [described as "sky-blue"] and a tail that stands on high when he is out on the parade ground. He is slow-moving. On cold days, he coughs an ominous cough. He sneezes and wheezes from asthma. He has glorious memories." The reporter also noted that Rags, as a dog Parisian born, came by his love of good French ice cream naturally.[3]

All this publicity moved Major Hardenbergh to subscribe to the Argus Press Clipping Bureau in New York as a way of gathering any Rags-related news that might have slipped the family's notice. But Rags's life from now on was not going to be just a series of old home week appearances at various postings among familiar faces. From being an almost sacred symbol of the great days of the First Division, Rags was about to be made to stand for something far more controversial. In 1925 soldiers from Fort Jay would enlist Rags as unwitting gatecrasher of an American institution then seen as sacrosanct: the dog show.

The American concept of a beauty pageant for dogs developed out of hunting culture imported from England.

From determining the perfect points of sight hounds, dog shows came to embrace only approved pedigreed breeds, their variety increasing as human interference created dogs as much fashion statements of a given season as the latest dress design, frequently with unfortunate organic and mental distortions matching the physical ones. In fact, the American mania for dogs as status symbols moved a British dog expert, Hugh Dalziel, to criticize as early as 1886 what he saw as dog fanciers' obsession with securing "a fame or notoriety through their dogs that they appear instinctively to know would be hopeless for them to seek in channels opened up by their [own] merits."[4]

Founded in 1876, the Westminster Kennel Club, named for the fashionable New York hotel where its founders met, has put on the oldest American dog show in continuous existence, making it the standard for all others to aspire to. Since 1877 the Westminster show has gone on every year without a hitch in New York City, first at the Hippodrome at Gilmore's Garden, then at Madison Square Garden starting in 1926. Only in the winter of 2014 (over 130 years later) did the Westminster Kennel Club Dog Show permit mixed breeds to compete in the arena, restricted to agility only. By contrast, in Great Britain, Crufts Exhibition, held yearly since 1891, began to recognize the merits of cross-breed dogs much earlier, launching a spin-off contest called Scruffts in 2001.

As at Westminster, at Scruffts cross-breed dogs are not judged on the criteria applicable to dogs of pedigree. Crossbred entrants are judged on how well they fulfill the requirements of several classes developed to reflect wider public interest. Thus Scruffts is not so much a contest of superiority (dogs are not judged on the "breed standard") as a democratic celebration of what people love best about a dog, ignoring its origins in favor of celebrating its character and accomplishments.

In a year marking the centenary of the start of the Great War, the 2014 Scruffts competition aptly included what can be described as a genuine war dog, though his battles were of a different sort from Rags's. A lanky, handsome stray of smoky brindle coat and trusting brown eyes, Wylie, as he was later named, is an Afghan *kuchi*, or herding dog, who lived (to use a charitable word) in the streets of Afghanistan's second largest city, Kandahar. His first rescue came thanks to the compassion of British soldiers based outside the city. Coming upon a street disturbance, the soldiers realized it was a mob of Afghan men beating the four-year-old dog with sticks. The soldiers were shocked but not surprised. A segment of Afghan (and broader Islamic) culture does consider dogs to be ritually unclean, but scripture said to enshrine this has been misinterpreted, according to Pen Farthing. A former Royal Marine commando who founded Nowzad, the Kabul-based charity that rescues dogs like Wylie, Farthing refers to a passage in the Hadiths (sayings of Mohammed) that recommends punishment for anyone "keeping" a dog. "In fact," writes Farthing, "the Prophet was actually simply stating that it was wrong to confine a dog, which as a social animal, needs the company of others." There was another and possibly more trenchant factor, Farthing points out: "the turmoil that Afghanistan had been through in the last forty years." It was a nation where "it was not unusual to find at least two generations of uneducated adults in any family," a record that was not improved by the restrictions imposed by the Taliban. Poor education and poor standards of health and hygiene led to a not irrational fear of rabies, which did the common street dog no favors. While rabies was a concern of foreign troops also, Wylie sought out their companionship at checkpoints, knowing he was safer there than anywhere else.[5]

Wylie had already survived being used as bait for the dog-fighting contests that are an ancient part of Afghan tradition, but the street beating had brought him close to death. The soldiers carried Wylie into the base hospital, where a doctor who attended him thought he would die that night. But, like Rags after the car accident at Fort Benning, Wylie somehow survived. Once recovered, he had to be released: as was the practice during Rags's military exploits a century ago, dogs are still barred from military bases. But then Wylie was found again, this time with more heartrending injuries. An Australian soldier risked censure to bring the dog to Nowzad. In doing so, she, and the Afghan veterinary staff at Nowzad, saved his life. After he had recovered, Wylie was flown by Nowzad to the United Kingdom, where during his four-month quarantine in preparation for joining his soldier he was visited daily by Sarah Singleton of Somerset. She had learned of Wylie through social media. "I wanted to meet this incredibly brave little dog," she explains, "and apologize to him for the abuse and suffering he's been through at the hands of man." Singleton was especially moved by Wylie's persistently loving nature and his ability to trust humans, despite what humans had done to him. It had been planned for Wylie to move to Australia, but he failed to meet the strict import conditions. So Singleton offered to foster Wylie; ultimately, she adopted him, and seeing how well he was recovering, she decided to enter him in Scruffts. Singleton did so partly to tell his story but also to recognize the work of the charity that had saved him. Yet even she was amazed when this dog who, just three years earlier, was being abused to death on the streets of Kandahar was chosen out of a total of twelve hundred entrants as Scruffts Crossbreed Rescue Dog of the Year. It was a triumph for bravery over pedigree that would have been unthinkable in dog shows of the past century, like the one in which Rags was surreptitiously entered.[6]

Though he, too, had come out of a war zone, Rags knew none of the deliberate violence and cruelty that were inflicted on Wylie. After his rescue in Paris he had never known anything but adulation from soldiers, for whom his loyalty and sacrifice in war mattered more than his pedigree. However, members of an exclusive dog fanciers' organization, when faced with a mutt with nothing but a war record to recommend him, would view Rags's origins very differently.

Jack Rohan does not reveal which wise guy in the Sixteenth Infantry first brainstormed the notion of entering Rags in the Long Island Kennel Club show, held annually at the Twenty-Third Regiment Armory in Crown Heights, Brooklyn. The soldiers most keen on the plan went first to Major Hardenbergh, "who declined to have anything to do with it," writes Rohan, "but explained that he did not feel authorized to veto it, if the men of the division favored it."[7] The major added that he had doubts about how happy Rags would be to be made part of such an event. Apart from anything else, his age was a real concern. In 1925 Rags was assumed to be nearly ten years old and was possibly even older.

Enthused that Major Hardenbergh had not expressly forbidden Rags's participation in the dog show, the men next took the case to their officers. They, too, had their doubts. While it was a fact that Rags had been born, nobody knew exactly when, and they knew even less about his lineage, which, obviously, denoted eligibility for entrance in such contests. Even today, no one who examines photographs of Rags comes to the same conclusion about his apparent ancestry, except to agree that it was mixed terrier (and that his family tree possibly contained a strain of poodle). But even if his exact mixture were known, when Rags was born no one thought of adding his name and birthday to a canine genealogy. As the Governors Island cook allegedly advised him a day before he was taken to the Armory: "Rags, anybody can get into a war, but only your family can get you into a dog show."[8]

Rohan implies that neither Helen Hardenbergh nor her daughters were in favor of Rags being taken to the bench show. This type of dog show requires contestants to be displayed on benches for the duration of the event, the better to be reviewed by everyone, from judges to other breeders—a very high standard to set for a dog who had never been entered in any kind of contest and who was not a purebred. Like Major Hardenbergh, however, the Sixteenth Infantry held the belief that since Rags belonged to the First Division as a whole, their vote was trumped by the wishes of the division's men en masse. However, Helen insisted that before Rags was taken to the show, he should receive a bath. The *New York Times* reported on October 10 that though the men of Governors Island thought Rags was fine as is, "a rough-looking customer, with tangled coat, for all his friendly tail and soft eye," Helen Hardenbergh put him in a tub of soapy water for what was probably the first real scrub of his life. She stopped short of tying on a ribbon—that would have cost Rags any remaining face he might have still possessed before his adoring friends, the Governors Island collies.[9]

One of the soldiers prepared a sign measuring six feet tall. On it, in clear, handsome lettering and with the crimson insignia of the "Big Red One" (the crimson "1" emblazoned on the division's khaki shoulder badge) interspersed among the words, was inscribed a pocket history of Rags's and Donovan's wartime experiences:

RAGS

Famous Mascot of the 1st Div., A.E.F.

Service Chevrons VV Wound Chevrons V.

Rags is the only dog veteran who went through the entire world war and lived to tell the tale—if he could talk.

GASSED AT MEUSE-ARGONNE

Oct. 9-1918

He and Sergeant Donovan, who picked him up in Paris for the First Division, were found together in No Man's Land—both gassed and nearly dead. The gas destroyed Rags' left [*sic*] eye. The surgeon who rescued the two took them both back to the same hospital. Later they came back to the States on the same transport ship. Donovan has since gone west.

Rags then found a permanent home with Major R. W. Hardenbergh of the Inspector General's Office, Governors Island. The Major gives Rags a home . . . and claim to ownership.—Rags . . . the First Division.[10]

A photograph was staged with this placard to show Rags as he would be displayed at the Armory bench show. First, the sign was propped on a table set against the iron-railed porch of the Hardenbergh residence at Fort Jay. Rags was set on top of this table, surrounded by gas masks and tools from trench warfare that he would have known as battlefield mascot.

These were cheerless relics of Rags's war career, but as the *New York Times* reported, along with them Rags was reunited with a much happier reminder of his past: S.Sgt. George E. Hickman, the only other person alive who knew Rags from his street mutt days, was there also, "assigned to mount guard beside Rags" for the Armory show.[11]

Like Rags, Hickman had had plenty of ups and downs himself since Armistice Day. In a 1939 newspaper article, he was described as having "had more than one man's share of wounds and battle engagements."[12] Severely wounded at Cantigny in May 1918, he had fought straight through till the war's end; at some point before Armistice he had lost his own mascot, the bulldog Dick. In May 1919 Hickman was still in Europe and wrote to his sister from Selters, Germany, that he was relieved by the prospect of shipping home soon. As he told her, "Next month will make me two years of this, and believe me I have begun to feel like an old man, and the hardships I have seen is more to make the best of us feel that way." Hickman was not yet twenty-eight years old.[13]

What he had endured would be sufficient to excuse him for leaving the army behind, as many men did, but Hickman was in this for life. A year after he wrote his sister of his utter exhaustion, he was back with the troops, posted to Camp Zachary Taylor in Kentucky. By November 1926 Hickman was in the New York City area, where he married. Ten years later, the Hickmans were still in New York because it was there that the sergeant was interviewed for Rags's obituary.[14]

There are plenty of photographs of Rags with other soldiers. Many of these men had also known him in France during the war; some had actually seen action alongside him. But only when Rags was with Sergeant Hickman did he seem to have found his best buddy. He was relaxed and playful, the frisky pup he was when Hickman and Donovan scooped him off the street. One image of Hickman and the terrier in particular, which was reproduced in articles about Rags after his death, seems to say everything about their close connection. In the photo, taken around 1929, Hickman crouches beside Rags, whose paws are on Hickman's knee, head thrown back and mouth opened in midbark. Dressed in full uniform with medals and fourragère over his left shoulder, Hickman hugs Rags close while making sure that his cloth collar, showing his service chevrons, is visible for the lens.

Not only was this dog lovable, Hickman seems to be suggesting, but this dog was a hero, and the proofs must be on clear display.

When considering which members of the Sixteenth Infantry came up with the notion of entering Rags in a canine beauty pageant, however, we can be sure Hickman was not among them. With Hickman, there is a sense of protectiveness toward the terrier, as if the sergeant is guarding him against such misadventures as might befall an elderly dog among a lot of First Division rookies (whose motives Hickman, like Rags, would not have been especially prone to trust). No wonder Hickman volunteered to be Rags's handler.

Rohan notes that on the entry form for the show, the men from Fort Jay jotted Rags down as an "Irish terrier." Despite the fact that Rags's photograph had appeared in several New York newspapers, one of which somebody affiliated with the dog show surely must have run across, the fib was accepted without question. The Army Information Service, which seems to have been deeply involved in the scheme, reported to the *New York Times* that all "arrangements were completed with the show and Rags was all set."[15] At this point, Rohan's and the newspaper's accounts diverge. Rohan claimed that several Fort Jay veterans, glittering in their medals, showed up at the show with Rags. "There an entry-clerk looked him over and declined to accept him as

Irish," says Rohan. The men suggested he was Scottish (which was as absurd as suggesting he was Irish). When this was declined, the men asked why Rags couldn't simply be entered as a war dog.

Unfortunately, the mindset of twenty-first-century Scruffts honoring heroic war dog Wylie was a very long way from that of 1925 Brooklyn. At that time, there was not a dog exhibition on earth that seriously considered allowing mixed-breed dogs to compete at all. This was one of the few attempts to enter a dog in a show solely on the basis of its war record. Admitting that he "regretted it," the Long Island Kennel Club clerk stated that Rags was not eligible for entry. As a result, "a dejected group of soldier-men drove slowly back to Governors Island," wrote Rohan.[16]

Rags's loss was magnified, at least to the soldiers with him, by the presence in the show of a blue ribbon–winning bulldog, Jiggs (II), who was purchased by boxing star and former Marine Gene Tunney to replace an earlier mascot of the Marines, Jiggs I. However, Rags harbored no hard feelings against Jiggs. They later met at Governors Island in 1927, where "they glanced at one another with a light in their eyes which the officers present took to be patriotism, and they became friends." When Jiggs died not long afterward, Rags was photographed gazing mournfully at a portrait of his pal.[17]

The New York Times painted a very different picture of the events around Rags's carefully planned conquest of the Long Island Kennel Club Dog Show. "At 10 o'clock Thursday night [before the show]," the paper was told by contacts at Fort Jay, "a telephone message came from the American Kennel Club, transmitted through Secretary Rohrbach of the Long Island Kennel Club, [which] barred Rags." The reason given was that no dog not accepted for entry in the show was allowed to be in the Armory. Evidently realizing this was not a satisfactory explanation, a show official named Joseph J. Connell "said later he thought Rags would have been welcomed as a hero" and that to his knowledge Rags *had* been included in the program. We will never know the truth. Evidently, like the men of Fort Jay, Connell wrongly assumed that a war hero had as much right to appear at a dog show as a dog who was no hero at all—aside, that is, from every show dog's heroic fortitude in patiently enduring being on constant public display. Like animals of war, show dogs have no choice.[18]

The Army Information Office wasted no time spreading the news of Rags's rejection to all corners of the continent. "The indignation against the barring of Rags became epidemic," wrote Rohan. Those who had doubted that he would be included in the show evidently had not really believed that: now they were the most vociferous of Rags's defenders. First Division veterans who had been leading relatively quiet lives now burst forth with heated letters of opinion to newspaper editors. Rohan added, "[Rags] was the center of a storm of controversy." Based on the public response, it's clear that Rags's case had stirred up a hornet's nest of latent animosity against the haughty restrictions of dog show tradition.[19] "Messages of condolence poured in from all parts of the country," stated the *New York Herald Tribune*. "Dog shows in states far distant wired for permission to have Rags entered as an exhibit." Major Hardenbergh declined to send him, stating that Rags was too old to bear up under the strain of so much travel. One woman, a Miss Frances Campion of New York, was moved by Rags's rejection to send a check for $25 "to get him a nice warm blanket and something to eat especially good." Rags and Major Hardenbergh posed for a photograph in which Rags, sitting on the major's knee, seems to be smiling toward the check his guardian is holding out for him to see. The reporter noted that Rags would return the check "with a note of thanks and a warm spot in his heart for the sender who would love a little dog for what he has done and not for what his family might be."[20]

The First Division was not to be mollified by Joseph Connell's apology. One newspaper gleefully reported that the army would ensure that Rags "is to have a show all his own. Governors Island announced yesterday that Rags would be the centre of the division's reunion to be held Oct. 24 at Fort Hamilton." Added the *New York Herald Tribune*, "Instead of a blue-blood show, it will be a red-blood show. Pedigrees are not to be barred, but they will not count. Actual achievement only will matter."[21]

The Governors Island men, like most military personnel bitter over congressional cutbacks to the armed services throughout the 1920s and 1930s while civilian high society spent fortunes on such amusements as the exhibition of purebred dogs, had not succeeded in crashing the pearly gates of Park Avenue. However, they did manage to reach into the heart of exclusive American show dog culture and awaken the pangs of its conscience. A year later, wrote Rohan, the Long Island Kennel Club issued an invitation to Rags to take part as a guest in the 1926 exhibition at the Twenty-Third Regiment Armory. This time, "a special class had been created for him," wrote Rohan. "Rags came away with the ribbon of the 'War-dog sweepstakes championship.'"[22] It is not impossible that the death of Sergeant Stubby that year (on March 16, estimated to be around eleven years of age), with obituaries run in newspapers across the nation and a taxidermied Stubby himself soon displayed in shop windows, sensitized the American Kennel Club to the "hero class" to which mascots like Stubby and Rags belonged. Or perhaps it was simply seen as politic to join in a new fashion of more flexible and nuanced appreciation from which dog show folk had hitherto held themselves strictly apart.[23]

But however much the Kennel Club's gesture was appreciated, and however many more medals were to be hung around his reluctant neck, Rags had progressed well past the trivialities of rosettes and contests. He had become a bona fide symbol of the determination and grit that had carried him through three battles in France and that now made him shine in peacetime. And no silk ribbon could ever match an honor of that caliber.

"A year ago, when it was discovered that [Rags] had been born rather than bred," stated the *New York Times*, "he was excluded from an imposing array of high-grade dog shows." But now he was the most eligible war dog in New York, photographed so often, according to one report, that he held the world record for dogs. By the time Rags received an invitation from the New York Junior League, he was prepared to accept and "was a decided success."[24]

The newspaper would have its readers imagine a drawing room full of debutantes and their mammas, cooing over a scruffy mongrel, but in fact the Junior League was (and continues to be) full of women of sturdy and serious purpose who understood exactly what Rags had done for his adopted country. Junior League members had been active since 1901 in a wide variety of volunteer, humanitarian-based roles. During the Great War, when Rags and Donovan were dodging whizz-bangs in

France, women from the league were serving volunteer hours in YMCA canteens and with the Red Cross, as well as selling Liberty bonds and assisting in countless other war efforts. Junior League members may have met Rags at Fort Sheridan in 1919, when women from the Chicago branch visited the hospital wards, bringing gifts and singing Christmas carols to the men. Shortly before the New York Junior League took Rags under its wing, it had taken charge of running a shelter for babies and the mothers who could not have otherwise afforded to keep them—a socially advanced stance for a group of society women a little over two decades past the heyday of Victorian rules of social conduct. Many of those who cared about the health and welfare of children and women also cared about the health and welfare of animals. During the war, Junior Leagues across the country were involved with the Red Star, the organization created in 1916 by the American Humane Association to afford aid to animals injured in battle.[25]

The Junior League invited Rags to partake of another honor. He was to be celebrated at an event honoring "Famous Pets of Famous People" at the Waldorf Astoria Hotel in Manhattan. The Governors Island men were thrilled, but they had been chastened by the experience of entering Rags in the Brooklyn dog show under false pretenses. Now they were so obsessed with making sure all the entry form lines were filled in accurately that they needed to lean on the leadership of Brig. Gen. Hugh A. Drum. One section of the entry form required that Rags's owner be named. Even Major Hardenbergh was reluctant to make that claim, as he saw himself merely as caretaker of the terrier on behalf of the First Division. So General Drum took his pen, "and with many breathless soldiers watching over his shoulder," he wrote down the only ownership claim that everyone could agree on. Rags, General Drum penned, belonged to *all* Americans.[26]

Rags continued to pay the price of prominence with a whole series of such public appearances, always covered by the New York papers. There was much excitement over the eighth anniversary of the first shot fired by American forces in the Great War (October 23, 1917). Naturally, Fort Hamilton was the setting for ceremonies involving both the Sixteenth and Eighteenth Infantries, "commanders, past and present, and the famous divisional mascot, Rags," to celebrate the occasion.[27] Most of the day's schedule was taken up with battle re-creations chosen from the Civil War and the Spanish-American War, in which both regiments had fought with distinction. Whether Rags was happy with all the mock shot and shell is not reported (Helen Hardenbergh claimed he was afraid of the booming of the evening gun at Governors Island), but one part of the day made him a very happy mascot. For the occasion, a glittering collection of officers had been gathered: Maj. Gen. Robert E. Bullard, Maj. Gen. Charles P. Summerall, Maj. Gen. Frank Parker, and Brig. Gen. Preston Brown.[28] Of course, there were reporters on hand, standing at the parade ground nearest the brassiest of the officers, whose adjutants fended off any untoward enquiries of the great men. At that moment, wrote Rohan, Rags "galloped down and, to the dismay of several junior officers, bounded up to a short, slim soldier in the uniform of a major-general. Before the juniors could tear him away, the general was scratching [Rags's] head and talking to him." Maj. Gen. Charles P. Summerall did the scratching. And though man and dog had not laid eyes on each other since Vaucouleurs in August 1918, when Rags had saluted Summerall outside camp headquarters, and though Rags now had just one good eye, they apparently knew each other on sight.[29]

A newsman asked whether Summerall and the other generals present would be interested in being photographed with Rags. Bullard was enthused; the others genially concurred. Sergeant Hickman, again in charge of Rags, clipped on his lead and readied him for the portrait while others fetched the six-foot signboard.

With the sign held up by two soldiers, Hickman positioned Rags, looking slightly bashful, on a plain wooden chair planted in parade ground grass strewn with crisp autumn leaves. To Rags's right stood Major General Bullard, formal in his civilian hat, coat, and tie, with Dr. Guy Shirey, General Bullard's medical officer during the Great War, to his right. To Rags's left, alongside Sergeant Hickman, stood uniformed Major General Summerall and Major General Parker. Rohan tells us that one of the younger officers chose this moment to joke that it looked as if the men were posing for a portrait of generals with a dog, rather than, he seemed to suggest, what should be a portrait of a dog with generals. Bullard quickly bristled. "Why not?" he barked back.

As Rohan claimed, the resulting photo was "probably the only one in which an army dog was given the position of honor by the highest ranking general officers in the army."[30]

But Rags already knew where he stood in the hierarchy of these officers' and soldiers' hearts.

No one ever forgot the time when, for the First Division's eleventh annual reunion at Fort Hamilton, Rags was observed taking another role normally reserved for a person of honor. "With his joints creaking from many months spent in the trenches, his gas-cough a little worse and his one eye less alert," wrote a reporter, Rags sauntered into General Drum's office, "the first overseas veteran to return for the reunion." Under typical circumstances, this presentation before the reunion would have gone to a human soldier of distinguished service. The writer notes, tongue in cheek, that as a ten-year veteran, Rags should have been aware of this rule. But General Drum made him welcome, his transgression not just ignored but tossed out the window. "Rags's venerable hairs," noted the reporter, "raise him above such matters."[31]

Yet Rags's venerable hairs didn't mean he was content to put aside the laddish wanderlust of his younger years. For the November 1929 reunion at Fort Hamilton, he displayed this propensity for random roving, unconcerned with any human plans that this activity might derail, in particularly spectacular fashion.

"It was the tenth gathering," wrote Rohan, "since the men of Meuse-Argonne, Soissons and other hot battles had been mustered out. . . . Arrangements were made for a sham battle—a reproduction of one of the hot moments of the old days."[32] In fact, the battle was a replay of a Meuse-Argonne action, the capture of the town of Exermont, with which Rags would have been very familiar, as it had occurred not long before he and Donovan were wounded. For the "three-day fete," ran an article on November 1, "several thousand veterans of the heroic First Division of the AEF assemble[d] [at Fort Hamilton] today."[33] A photo run along with the article showed Rags being steadied as he stood on the barrel of a 75 mm gun, his blind eye turned blankly toward the camera, a rippling enthusiasm making every hair on his body stand on end.

Rags had always enjoyed divisional reunions before, or so it seemed to the people who organized them. So his absence was puzzling, and frustrating, since it was Rags's presence that had ensured that the reunion was mentioned at all in the New York papers. The fall of 1929 was a difficult time for everyone, and it was well nigh impossible to gain the attention of newsroom editors preoccupied with the stock market, which had crashed a few days earlier. Only the fact that during the practice runs for the reunion Rags had been rescued at the last minute from an oncoming car, in full view of everyone, including a policeman who then leaked the incident to the press, was the reunion given any newsprint traction. Without Rags, even with such a prestigious guest as General Summerall, there didn't seem much point even holding a reunion. Rags was living up to a description given of him by a newspaper reporter who followed his comings and goings. Rags, wrote the reporter, was "a terrier of considerable personal independence."[34]

Several newspapers exploited the mystery by putting out alerts regarding the mascot's disappearance. "Rags is a casualty, a prisoner, or AWOL," noted the *New York Daily News*, reporting that Rags had gone missing "a few hours before taps" (ten o'clock in the evening) on October 31. "The entire outfit and depot brigade mobilized to search for him under Maj. Raymond W. Hardenbergh." Phone calls went out to all forts or other military installations through the area, asking everyone to be on the lookout for the terrier. "A landing party combed Bedloes Island [on which the Statue of Liberty stands]. Even General Charles P. Summerall and Brig. Gen. Hugh A. Drum . . . took a hand in looking for Rags." The clerk for the county of Queens, Edward W. Cox, offered a reward of $250—no small sum for the time—to anyone who could bring Rags back to Fort Hamilton.[35] "Some old timer who knew him in France may have taken him for a joke," said Major Hardenbergh, clearly upset, "but it's no joke to us. The dog is very old, and if he got in traffic he might be killed."[36]

So where did Rags go to on this infamous occasion?

Rohan gives his version of Rags's adventures over those two days. He claims the near miss with the car at Fort Hamilton had scared Rags so much that he found his way to the dock and onto a mine-planter that he knew, from past sailings, would bring him back to Governors Island. There, a couple of Sixteenth Infantry sergeants ran into him and, having heard about the near tragedy with the car, concluded that Rags didn't want to be around all the fuss, or around the Eighteenth Infantry, and that if Rags didn't want to be at Fort Hamilton, he shouldn't have to go back there. Rags spent that night at Governors Island. Rohan says the men then carried Rags to Fort Wadsworth (on Staten Island) the next day, November 2, by which time they realized from news reports that there was a serious search on for the dog and many upset people, including fearsome General Summerall. The reward money was tempting, Rohan says, but it wasn't worth a court martial. Back to Fort Hamilton went Rags the following day.

Rohan's story doesn't accord with the *New York Times*' version, which was published on November 3, describing Rags's return a day before Rohan claims it occurred. The article states simply that Rags, who had vanished a few days before, had come back to Fort Hamilton from wherever lost dogs go, in time to enjoy the fête and the good eating that was to be had. It is just as possible that Rags, rather than being spirited off to Staten Island and wherever else rumor placed him, simply did one of the runners he had done on many a battlefield and military base.

In the comparative quiet of Brooklyn, he may have found a generous cook or two at kitchen doors, possibly a place to stay that was off the beaten track. Not everybody would have necessarily recognized "the most photographed dog in the world." Rags may have slept most of the time, or maybe he wandered alleyways, reliving his street dog days while he had a chance to do so, away from the sound and fury of Fort Hamilton and unwanted attention. And perhaps, after seeing all the familiar veterans from his past, he was looking for another familiar face, one that he hadn't seen for ten years. "Dogs really *do* miss their owners when they are separated from them," writes John Bradshaw. Yet there is a downside to this intensity of love, he says. Coupled with a dog's powerful memory, even of a human it loved years before, it may "find it difficult to cope without us." Perhaps Rags's way of coping was to head off somewhere, sniffing the ground and the air for the familiar aroma of the soldier who had been his first and best love.[37]

On his reappearance at Fort Hamilton, Rags was described as slinking around the parade ground at first, as if contrite about having taken French leave. He was seen "looking none too happy, until the first shots from the field guns and the first Verey-lights [flare guns] from no-man's land recalled other days and made [him] prance about to the delight of the veterans."[38] Rohan agrees that when Rags returned and saw what he had been missing, he raced into the middle of the action, as reported, "then dashed to the side of the foremost soldier on the left flank," just as, it was presumed, he had done with Sergeant Donovan in France. At the conclusion of the exercise, Rohan says, all the soldiers "clustered around [Rags], scratched his back, and patted him. 'Great work,' they told him. 'You're one swell little soldier yet.'" He was also a swell little actor. "When the [Hardenbergh] family arrived" at their Hamilton lodgings that afternoon, worn out with worry over where Rags could be, Rohan adds, "they found him waiting for them on the porch, still looking meditative, and puzzled."[39]

In 1928 Raymond Hardenbergh was posted to the War College in Washington DC.

Rohan jibes that the college was "an unusual sort of school . . . where virtually all the students have graying hair" and where "a certain schoolboy spirit pervades the place."[40] He may have had it right. At the time Major Hardenbergh was at the Army War College (incidentally, at the same time as Maj. Dwight D. Eisenhower), the college was much as Rohan describes, "a pleasant, contemplative assignment for senior professionals of that generation," as Dr. Benjamin Franklin Cooling III describes it. Another commentator explained that the college seemed "contrived for a leisurely respite." After often long careers spent organizing the lives of men below them and being organized by men above them, officers at the War College had a rare opportunity to let down their guard, if only for the duration of a course. This would prove an ideal atmosphere for Rags.[41]

The Hardenberghs lived off the campus, but with so many officers aware of the presence of the hero dog of the First Division and that atmosphere of leisurely respite, Rags often went to the college on his rambles. He was allowed to do so, despite the Hardenberghs' discouragement and the more serious obstacle of municipal regulations barring unmuzzled dogs from War College property. In fact, Rohan says this regulation extended to all public parks in the District of Columbia. The War College officers' habit of looking the other way as Rags trotted about the campus gave him tacit permission to wander without muzzle everywhere else, including Potomac Park in Washington itself.

Rohan does not indicate which Potomac Park this was. The War College was located at what is now Buzzard Point on the Anacostia River. East Potomac Park lies to the west across the Washington Channel. West Potomac Park lies north of there, south of the Lincoln Memorial on the banks of the Tidal Basin. There is one route Rags could have taken to East Potomac Park, but it is located so close to West Potomac Park that he could just as easily have gone there, as both parks are many blocks northwest of the college. East Potomac Park may well be the one Rohan means, as it had been the site of temporary army barracks during the Great War and had a teahouse and other amenities that could have attracted Rags's inveterate bent toward mooching. Whichever park it was, it was there that Rags was apprehended by a motorcycle policeman who noticed that he was not wearing a license tag—it had been lost recently and not replaced. So Rags was taken back to the police station, where his collar plate was examined by the men.

The police captain had served in the war and on seeing "First Division Rags" recalled hearing about the dog and his keeper, Donovan. Assuming this was the same division mascot, the captain also assumed that Donovan was still living somewhere nearby. (Apparently no one noticed the name "Major Hardenbergh" on the tag.) It was too late in the afternoon to call military authorities to confirm, so the captain ordered Rags taken out to the sidewalk. But when he was told to go home, Rags padded back into the station. While the captain was again urging Rags forward, and Rags was responding by not budging, a figure out of American military history appeared on the scene. The captain immediately stood to salute Gen. John J. Pershing, who was walking his round a bit later than usual.[42] General Pershing was now in his late sixties but was still a dapper man who "carried a blackthorn stick and strode along like a man of fifty," Rohan wrote. The general lived in the elegant Wyoming Apartments flat of his good friend Francis E. Warren, the elderly senator from Wyoming. (Pershing later moved to an apartment in the Carlton Hotel.) Pershing had never learned to drive. Since riding a horse was out of the question, he took his exercise with a daily walk about town.[43]

Seeing Rags sitting in confusion on the sidewalk, Pershing asked what was the matter. The captain explained that this was First Division Rags, adding that as they didn't know where Sergeant Donovan lived, they were trying to get the dog to go home to him of his own volition. This reference to a soldier by then dead ten years may have taken the general back to the day in 1919 at the Château du Val des Écoliers, when he sat in his dressing gown trying to read his Memorial Day speech to his aide, Quekmeyer, losing his composure as he thought of all the young men lying under the sod of the Meuse valley. Rohan says the old man quickly set the police straight: Donovan had died years ago; did no one read the papers anymore? As for Rags, "Dog's on the retired list, like myself," Rohan has Pershing say. The captain ventured to ask whether Pershing knew where the dog's current owner lived. Pershing replied he didn't know but had heard that "Major So-and-So" was at the War College; that's where he would drop Rags off. Hailing a cab, Pershing put Rags on the back seat, got in himself, and directed the driver to the college. On arriving, the general set the terrier on the sidewalk, and with an emphatic "Go home, Rags," directed the driver to his home on Connecticut Avenue. According to Rohan, he was still unwilling to just leave Rags to his own devices. Rohan claims Pershing asked the driver to slowly trail the dog until they could see Rags safely reach the gate.[44]

Shortly after his encounter with Pershing, Rags began manifesting behaviors that were taken note of by the War College men. He was a dog who lived by the creed according to which all curiosity must be satisfied, no matter the distance he had to travel to do so. But now he seemed not so much curious as desperate, Rohan reported. Each day he nosed his way into every office and up to every unfamiliar officer, as if in search of something or someone. It dawned on everybody that Rags was probably looking for the old general—or maybe he was looking for the First Division itself, that first and dearest family that had taken him in.

When a convoy of First Division trucks from Governors Island cruised into the War College grounds at this time, Rags was seen nosing around one of the trucks. He jumped into it, where he found a saddle, bridle, and blanket that Pershing had gifted to the captain in charge of the convoy. Rohan claims that it was as if Rags already knew the saddle was there. On locating it, "with a running leap, [Rags] landed aboard" and sniffed the kit all over. He was spotted lying on the blanket, but by the time the trucks were started up and on the move north, he had been forgotten. But not for long. The drivers had planned an all-nighter, reaching Fort Jay in time for breakfast. However, somewhere south of Trenton, the journey came to a halt when the driver of the truck containing Pershing's saddle was startled to hear barking. The men pulled over, saw that Rags had hitchhiked with them, knew it was too late to turn back, and so made the best of the delay by breakfasting with him on army rations. Once they had reached Governors Island, Rags went gaily about greeting his friends both human and canine; "in a few minutes," wrote Rohan, "there was a ring of soldiers around Rags, patting him, scratching him, and telling him what a fine dog he was."[45] Then a pilot who had been granted a forty-eight-hour leave pass off the island strapped Rags into an amphibious plane, and they set off for Washington. High in the air for the first time since his balloon ride at Saint-Mihiel in 1918, Rags is said to have been similarly unimpressed with flight: he lay down and slept until the plane came to a bobbing stop on the Anacostia River. Back on land, Rags "started across the grounds as nonchalantly as if he was returning from a mere constitutional trot around the block."[46]

In his account of his friendship with Strongheart, canine movie star of the 1920s, J. Allen Boone writes that the German shepherd "always made the immediate occasion and the immediate circumstance yield some kind of dividend in interest and fun." Where Rags was concerned, Rohan would surely have agreed, noting that "one way or another, [Rags] managed to break up the monotony of life, not only for himself, but for his friends." In helping people realize that for all its wars between nations and between people, the world was still a beautiful place, Rags proved himself a soldier not just of war but of love. The good cheer and inspiration he dispensed just by existing would soon make him the subject of the first full-length biography of a genuine dog of the Great War.[47]

10

Old Warrior

For those, O Lord, the humble beasts, that bear with us the burden
and heat of the day, and offer their guileless lives for the well-being
of mankind; and for the wild creatures, whom Thou hast made wise,
strong, and beautiful, we supplicate for them Thy great tenderness
of heart, for Thou hast promised to save both man and beast and
great is Thy loving kindness, O Master, Savior of the world.

—GUY VERNON SMITH, *The Bishop of London's Visit to the Front*

We can guess why, but we don't know just when Jack Rohan was moved
to write his biography of Rags.

Rohan was in the area around Chicago in 1920, when Rags was the
mascot of Fort Sheridan (some eighty miles northeast of Morris); he
could well have heard of the dog through the military grapevine. He
must surely have become aware of his story through newspaper articles
appearing around the time Rags resurfaced at Governors Island. For all
we know, Rohan may have been commissioned to write the book by Major
Hardenbergh, whose active assistance is acknowledged by the author.

When he started on his project, Rohan would have been at least
acquainted with earlier recent books telling the stories of animals who
served and sacrificed in the Great War. There was Bertha Whittridge
Smith's *Only a Dog: A Story of the Great War*, the 1917 memoir of a French
terrier who bonds with and dies beside an American soldier in France. In
1920 came Col. Edwin H. Richardson's *British War Dogs: Their Training
and Psychology*, relating anecdotes about the dogs he trained and the
incredible acts of bravery they displayed. Five years later, Ernest Harold
Baynes's *Animal Heroes of the Great War*, the naturalist's masterpiece
celebrating all the animals known to have assisted in the war effort,
was published posthumously in New York City.

As far as books about the lives of individual dogs were concerned, Laurence Trimble's biography of Strongheart, the first canine movie star, was published in 1926, three years before the German Shepherd's untimely death. In 1928 Alexander Woolcott, the sharp-penned New York theater critic, published a loving essay about Verdun Belle, a white-and-brown setter rescued by a soldier. Belle served many of the battlefield roles Rags did, and one he did not: she gave birth to a litter of puppies, which her soldier master tried to save through a long march. Parted from each other and the soldier wounded, the soldier and Belle were reunited in a field hospital, where Belle refused to leave his side.

Though following the same general outline as these writers, with *Rags* Rohan was definitely doing something different with what had already become a sentimentalized topic.

For starters, Rohan made the decision not to write the book as an imagined memoir of a dog but as a chronicle of Rags's life, as close to the truth as verified anecdote and documented event could make it. Though there are no known photographs of Rags in France, Rohan used what the Hardenbergh family and the military were able to provide rather than an artist's imagined renderings; the only cartoonist's image of Rags ever used was in an advertisement of the book. Rohan also honorably refused all opportunities to name-drop. Other than identifying General Summerall and General Drum, along with Major Hardenbergh, Rohan resisted calling out General Pershing, Colonel Holbrook, or Colonel Dorey. Above all, of course, was the fact that no other officially recognized military mascot had had its life put into book form until Rohan, via interviews, letters, newspaper articles, and enough artistic license to hold it together, created *Rags*.

That the book's scenes are structured in a cinematic fashion comes as no surprise. Rohan probably had Hollywood in mind all along—and if he hadn't, somebody else would have, because by the time *Rags* appeared, animal movie stars had reigned supreme for several years. "By 1930," writes Mark Derr, "some 400 dogs were working in the film industry, the majority of them mongrels of the terrier type, trained on food or games."[1] The most famous of these dogs was Rin Tin Tin, a German shepherd saved from a battlefield by an American gunnery corporal, Lee Duncan of the 135th Aero Squadron. Duncan had had to leave a beloved dog behind when he signed up in 1917, as had more than a few soldiers (and, perhaps, as had Donovan), so he was in the right frame of mind after the Saint-Mihiel offensive to adopt the dog and puppies he found abandoned in a German kennel. That unlikely beginning, and the sheer dumb luck of one of the pups, whom Duncan named after a French doll called Rintintin, propelled the film career of the greatest canine star of the silent screen. Rinty, as Duncan nicknamed him, entered film at a special time in American history, one that was to have a similar magical effect on Rags as mascot of the First Division. It was an era when movies provided escape from a menacing real world to a sparkling larger-than-life fantasy for the measly price of a movie ticket. Americans still dazed from the stock market crash were distracted from reality by Busby Berkeley's kaleidoscopic dancing girls, elegant Fred and Ginger, slinky Joan Crawford, wacky Eddie Cantor. Though moviemaking was hardly a safe place for animals (onscreen deaths of horses and other animals prompted regular surveillance by the American Humane Association on movie sets as early as 1939), for human viewers the adventures of screen animals opened a door into a new and painless place, that of people's childhoods, or people's childhoods as they imagined or wanted them to be.

"People began dreaming about animals because animals reminded them of a more tender time," writes Susan Orlean, Rin Tin Tin's biographer. "But they also may have cared about animals more because they saw more clearly into their own lives."[2]

Many of those dreamers, to the tune of two hundred people, gathered one brisk November day in 1930 at Fort Hamilton to watch Rags pawtograph a copy of *Rags*.

Had Rags been younger and the Hardenberghs of a different mind, the Fort Hamilton event might have been just the first of a series of appearances, the prelude to a cross-country book tour, with Rags and Rohan hitting all the major army bases and cities between New York and San Francisco with a detour to Los Angeles for photo ops with Rin Tin Tin and Jean Harlow. That was not to be, and that was a good thing. The Hardenberghs had known Rags through many years of rambunctious activity, daring wanderings, near-death accidents, and energetic participation in all the daily business of military posts across the country. Now, like the soldiers who had known Rags in France, the terrier was growing old. The bustle and publicity around the Long Island Kennel Club show and the fright of Rags's disappearance from the 1929 reunion evidently moved the Hardenberghs to reduce his exposure to stressful situations.

In this, Rags was lucky, because as a celebrity animal in Depression-era America he was never exploited by the people who cared for him. For all their insistence that they were simply Rags's caretakers, and though there were public events (usually military related) that they did allow Rags to be part of, the Hardenberghs were people who prized their privacy. They knew that Rags, his gregariousness with his soldiers aside, also preferred quiet in the circle of his family. The Hardenberghs could easily have allowed Rags to become the canine equivalent of Shirley Temple, but they loved him too much to inflict on him the tiring demands of other people's affection.

For Rags's Fort Hamilton book launch, though, the Hardenberghs made an exception.

An event of this kind, along with the celebrated commanders who would be in attendance, would be seen as the ultimate fitting celebration of Rags's military career. So the Hardenberghs brought him over to Fort Hamilton for what promised to be a unique and moving event. And then Rags made clear just what *he* thought of the proceedings: he promptly disappeared.

The morning of the autograph ceremony, a table was set up on the Fort Hamilton parade ground lawn, on top of which Rags was meant to sit. Behind the table stood a platoon of soldiers, chins held at a jaunty angle. On the table lay a special leather-bound copy of *Rags*, together with an ink pad and pen. On one side of the table waited Brig. Gen. Lucius R. Holbrook, sleekly uniformed, on the other Jack Rohan in a three-piece suit. We know that General Holbrook was clearing his throat nervously, because not far from him stood Paul Harrison, a Newspaper Enterprises Association journalist who was taking down every detail of the awkward scene. "'Harr-rumph!' snorted the General," Harrison wrote, "who had waited longer than generals are supposed to wait for anybody. 'Where is the—ah—guest of honor?'"[3] A nearby colonel made an effort to mollify the general while at the same time looking to pass the hot potato of embarrassment elsewhere. Major Hardenbergh himself was nowhere to be seen; he had dashed off with a detachment to find Rags. Minutes ticked by as Harrison and the other reporters scribbled, adjutants worried about what they were writing, cameramen shuffled from one foot to another, and officers' wives made discreet small talk to fill the void.

"Just then," wrote Harrison, "a sergeant [Hickman?] came up at the double and deposited on a table an animate bundle of dirty fuzz that he had dug out of a coal bin."[4] Rags shook out the black dust that still clung to what could now be truthfully termed dirty-blond hair. Major Hardenbergh and his men returned, pausing a moment to straighten caps and uniforms. Then Hardenbergh took Rags's leash and placed his other hand over Rags's back—no sense having him misbehave further with all the press around.

Turning halfway to Rags and half toward his audience, General Holbrook took a breath and launched into his prepared remarks, to which Rags is said to have paid great attention, "[cocking] his one good ear as the General began to speak."[5]

Rags, after twelve years I am glad to see that you are still with the First Division as its mascot. We were together in France. I was your commander. You fought at Soissons and in the Argonne forest. I am told that you were also at St. Mihiel. I am told that your biography has been written, and I am proud that it will take its place in the Imperial War Museum beside the record of other heroes, marked with the print of the paw that was wounded in the Argonne.[6]

Rohan and Holbrook then made a gesture as extraordinary and touching as Summerall, Bullard, and Parker had done for their group portrait with Rags a few years earlier.

Normally, an officer of Holbrook's rank would remove his hat only on certain special occasions, such as when entering a place of worship, attending a formal indoor reception, or at the raising of the flag. For Rags's special day, Holbrook and Rohan both doffed their hats. With Rohan caressing Rags's head, Holbrook took the terrier's stiff right front paw. He pressed it onto the ink pad and placed the paw on the title page of the book. Though extremely disinclined to be present on this very public occasion—likely exacerbated by the applause that exploded as his paw touched the page—Rags left something resembling three toes and the pad of his foot in deep blue ink, a smudged but recognizable "signature." Following the applause, writer and soldier covered up again, and a photographer captured Rags looking trustingly up at General Holbrook, everyone around them smiling.

This signed copy of Rags's life story (Rohan having added his own signature and the words "The ink blots are the mark made by Rags with the paw wounded in action") was duly sent to the Imperial War Museum, whose librarian, H. Foster, had specifically requested it for the museum's collection. Rags, as usual, had a more philosophical approach to such fame as rarely attached itself to former street mutts from Paris. According to reports of the day, he jumped down from the table and ran back to the coal bin.[7]

A few months after the ceremony at Fort Hamilton, Rags was brought to New York City for another event. In his first appearance before the general public, Rags was to receive a medal from the American Anti-Vivisection Society (AAVS) at Wanamaker's Department Store at Broadway and Tenth.

Founded in Philadelphia in 1883, the AAVS had started as a means of establishing regulations around the use of animals in scientific research; later, it sought to stop the use of animals in live experiments entirely. The battle between the leaders of scientific discovery who believed animal experimentation the necessary key to finding new drugs and procedures to benefit humanity and laypeople with a horror of what they saw as needless torture continues to rage in our day, but the fight was hot long before Rags's lifetime. Diana Belais (1858–1944), who came to Wanamaker's Auditorium to give Rags his medal and induct him into the AAVS Legion of Hero Dogs, was one of the animal welfare movement's most uncompromising activists.

With her husband, David, Diana had spent most of her life standing up for what she believed was right, courting the same controversy as Henry Bergh, fellow New Yorker and founder of the American Society for the Prevention of Cruelty to Animals. Bergh, in fact, was an unlikely prototype for much modern-day animal welfare activism. A wealthy man who had been awakened by animal abuse he had witnessed in the streets of imperial Russia and the bullrings of Spain, Bergh was only Victorian by accident: in everything he did he would not have been out of place in the twenty-first century. Bergh wasn't content to sit at a desk or lobby legislators. He patrolled the streets of New York, publicly calling out horse drivers and abattoir operators for cruelty. He once caused a traffic jam several miles long when, on seeing the driver of an overloaded omnibus beat the exhausted horses, Bergh threw the driver into the snow and unhitched the horses, leaving the commuters to find their own way home.[8]

After Bergh's death, Diana and David Belais came to believe that the ASPCA had lost its keen edge, becoming less investigator and prosecutor and more an arm of the New York City municipal dog pound. The couple used their considerable wealth and connections to found the Humane Society of New York, incorporated in 1904. David Belais would go on to fight for and win a rare conviction of animal cruelty, based on a statute dating from the 1860s, of a New York vivisectionist, while Diana showed she had just as much chutzpah as her husband.

In April 1908, at a meeting of the Woman's Republican Club at the Plaza Hotel, Diana spoke to the group and their guests about bills to regulate vivisection that were then under review by the state legislature and that she had helped push through. The relatively sedate gathering suddenly became a battleground as three men, doctors "who somehow chanced to be present[,] pounced upon the speaker," reported the *New York Times*. As Diana tried to continue, the men shouted her down, so she took them on. "We should not be called anti-vivisectionists," Belais blazed, "but restrictionists." By this she meant that she and the AAVS intended not just to regulate but to bring the practice to a full stop. This threat stirred the physicians to denounce her further and caused the meeting to run far over its appointed time of adjournment.[9]

Obviously Diana Belais had a high regard for honor and principle held despite all odds, which is what made it especially fitting that it was she who stood on the stage of Wanamaker's Auditorium, Rags's medal in hand.[10]

Journalist Lorena Hickock was present for the event, which she described as consisting of "speeches and lots of applause." Wanamaker's impresario, Grover Whalen, made stirring remarks on Rags's "great war record, his patriotism, and his loyalty to the United States," while Diana Belais concentrated on his most recent honor of sending a personalized copy of his life story to London. Jack Rohan, in his element at an event both commercial and patriotic, took a comic approach. He asked Rags if he had anything he wanted to say, which raised laughter from the crowd.[11] Then Miss Helen Hardenbergh held Rags in place as Diana Belais hooked the Legion of Hero Dogs medal onto his collar, followed by more applause.

To Hickock, Rags appeared rather blasé about it all. "All this fuss incident to [the medal's] bestowal bored him not a little," she reported. "But Rags was a gentleman. Gravely courteous, he permitted small boys and girls with flushed cheeks and shining eyes to crowd round him and pat him in the wrong places." She added that Rags only let slip his unflappable courtesy twice—once when he fidgeted on the table, and again when the flashes from the cameras made him drop down on his belly, as he had once done when bombs blasted over the war-torn trenches of France.[12]

The ceremony at Wanamaker's, with all its photographers, reporters, reaching children, and schedule tiring for a dog his age, was Rags's last appearance at a public event designed especially around him. That he was aging rapidly is evident in an article published in late 1933 or early 1934. The reporter, who seems to have met Rags, noted that "his once brown and fuzzy coat is getting gray and thin." He also noted that the terrier was completely deaf. As Rags slept on his bed in the kitchen near the warmth of the stove, "the Hardenberghs hear him yipping softly now and then, and know Rags is dreaming of thrilling days and gallant deeds in France." We humans assume that when a dog dreams, it is reliving or imagining the chase of a squirrel or another dog from earlier that day. But in Rags's case the reporter may have been closer to the truth than he realized. "Since we know that emotions are closely linked to dreams," writes Jeffrey Masson, "we can assume that a dog with good memories also has complex dreams laden with emotion."[13] Certainly, if there was ever a dog laden with emotions and memories, it was Rags. And as his years caught up with him, it was during sleep that he best caught up with his past in a present that increasingly slowed him down.[14]

When Rags did begin to age, it showed all too clearly. In a family photograph from 1933, Rags is captured standing alongside the Hardenberghs' new Ford, and though his tail is up and his ears alert, the reflection of him from behind, seen in the shiny car door, betrays a body bony with age. Another, later photo shows Raymond Hardenbergh sitting on a porch with Rags standing beside him. Promoted to lieutenant colonel and close to his own retirement from military service, Hardenbergh has hair that looks silver in the sunshine; so, too, does that of the small dog to his left, over whose thin body Hardenbergh curves a protective arm. Rags's coat is scruffy and tangled; he has the appearance of an aged person who is tired and confused. He looks as if he would be happier out of the sunlight and asleep under the stove, where dreams could not drain him as much as a brief walk out to the porch.

Rags's last known public outing occurred in May 1935. He had been brought to Governors Island for a polo match between players from the island and from the New York Athletic Club. But Rags's days as a crowd-pleaser were over. He lay resting beside Helen Hardenbergh, content to watch as a young fox terrier named Sherry "provided amusement for the fans during the half-time intermission by exhibiting his prowess as a golf-ball retriever [on the polo field]."[15]

Shortly after the game, the Hardenberghs packed up once again, taking their furniture and Rags back to Washington DC.

11

The Dog That Had a Soul

In 1920 a couple named Richard and Bertha Birney purchased a ten-acre parcel in Montgomery County, Maryland, not quite five miles east of Rockville. The land had once formed a small part of a seventeenth-century tract called Hermitage, a word for retreat or sanctuary that would be most fitting for what the Birneys planned to do with their property: creating one of the foremost, and most controversial, pet cemeteries in the United States.[1]

Described as a "florid-faced man with a ready tongue," Richard Conway Birney came of an American background with just as much history as the land he had purchased at 13630 Georgia Avenue.[2]

Born on August 10, 1876, in Washington DC, Birney was the eldest son of Arthur Alexis Birney, attorney for the District of Columbia, assistant U.S. attorney, and Howard University law professor, and Helen Townsend Conway.[3] Through his father, Birney had a cousinship with the family of President James Madison; through his mother, to the maternal Ball relatives of President George Washington.[4] He came from a line of movers and shakers, most prominent of them being his great-grandfather James Gillespie Birney (1792–1857), slave owner turned leading abolitionist at a time when animal welfare and abolition of slavery went hand in hand in the minds and activism of many reformers.[5]

The area where the Birneys' property lay was considered rural, though it was accessible via a short drive from the nation's capital. Like many of the tracts thereabouts it had been oriented toward farming; in fact, in the 1920 census, Birney described himself as a farmer.[6] But that was not why the Birneys had bought the land. They were breeders of pedigreed dogs. The Birneys first bred Boston terriers, a popular dog in the United States in the years before and after the Great War.

As public tastes altered in favor of other breeds, the Birneys expanded their kennels to include Scottish terriers and miniature schnauzers.[7]

The Birneys named their business Aspin Hill Kennels, using a spelling that still confuses people who assume the place was named for Aspen Hill Road, which abuts the property to the north. According to tradition, the Birneys adopted the name from kennels they had admired in England. Where they got the idea for an animal cemetery, however, is unclear. Birney's father was born in France, and it is possible that at some point in his youth Birney had been to Paris, where he may have visited the Cimetière des chiens et autres animaux domestiques (opened in 1899 in Asnières-sur-Seine), a renowned and romantic burial place not just for pet dogs but for animals of all kinds. It is sometimes alleged that this cemetery gave Richard Birney the idea for starting a place of his own in which to honor deceased pets. But it is also said that Birney and his wife were moved to do so by a visit to the Hartsdale Pet Cemetery in the New York town of that name. There may be more truth to this. Founded in 1896, Hartsdale was the first pet cemetery to be opened in the United States. Much about its layout resembles what the Birneys created at Aspin Hill, just as much about how it started mirrors what happened at Aspin Hill: a veterinarian who owned an apple orchard on the site allowed the guardian of a deceased dog to bury it there. The Birneys' cemetery began with their own need for a place to bury their dogs and, in time, the pets of their close friends. By 1921 the circle had widened, and the cemetery was a growing concern, as many people began to pay the Birneys to inter their pets at Aspin Hill.[8]

A brochure for the Birneys' cemetery survives. From the text of the brochure it can be seen that the Birneys, aside from their real love for animals, were also aware of the business potential of their venture:

Aspin Hill Cemetery for pet animals was opened to the public in 1921 in response to an urgent and insistent demand for a fitting place of this kind near the Nation's Capital, where the owners of faithful pets could feel assured of a permanent well-kept resting place for their real friends.

The Cemetery is the fulfillment of a need that pet owners and lovers of animals have felt for many years. It is the only accredited cemetery of its kind in the south and is rapidly becoming nationally known; visitors from many distant states inspect it annually. Authorities on the subject now credit it as one of the most attractive in the United States, and because of its proximity to Washington, the Nation's Capital, it is destined to become, in time, one of the noted canine cemeteries of the world.[9]

By 1930, when *American Motorist* magazine was touting Aspin Hill as "the fourth largest cemetery to be found for animals anywhere," news of which "is spreading fast, and cars bearing tags from many states stop at the entrance," the Birneys had the wherewithal to build a Tudor Revival bungalow at the east end of their property. The gabled red-brick house boasted a massive stone fireplace in a corner of the living room, with wooden beams supporting the ceilings. The couple was also able to employ two live-in servants.[10]

Throughout the 1920s, Aspin Hill began to fill with stone tablets marking the graves of pet burials, just as the fields surrounding the property began to sprout houses. Most were small and unadorned, with the name and dates of the animal carved on the front and the guardian's family name at the top edge; these stones cost anywhere from $25 to a rich $250.[11] Some of the graves bear memorials on a human scale—a rock-walled, iron-gated mausoleum for a Boston terrier named Mickey, for example (the ashes of his human guardians are interred in front of his tomb), or elaborate sculptures of dogs and cats, as well as marble or granite plinths inset with enameled plaque portraits of the deceased. In time, the dogs of noted personages like J. Edgar Hoover, director of the FBI, would be buried at the cemetery. As at Hartsdale, Aspin Hill was to inter all kinds of animals. By 1938 there were an estimated 2,600 burials: "dogs, horse, canaries, cats, and even raccoons," wrote a visiting journalist. "A white rabbit that used to follow its master like a dog was given a free burial because its bereaved little boy had no money." By then, some twenty-nine humans were buried there as well.[12]

In 1931, when World Animal Day was founded on the feast day of Saint Francis to recognize the plight of endangered species and later to honor all animals everywhere, Birney began giving public talks to crowds that gathered at Aspin Hill. These people were guardians of pets interred at the cemetery or those who supported the cause, or they were just road tourists who wanted to see the kooky animal cemetery they had heard about. While Birney, his head bared, stood amid graves "garnished with peonies, rose bushes, cut flowers, and other remembrances from bereaved owners," eulogizing the celebrated and the everyday among the deceased dogs buried in his cemetery, the living dogs in his audience, recalled one journalist, "engaged in scattered skirmishes, accompanied by biting, barking and yipping."[13]

Today Hardenbergh family members are unsure as to how Rags came to live with Richard and Bertha Birney. One theory is that when the Hardenberghs moved into their apartment on Wyoming Avenue in Washington, they were unable to keep Rags due to the terms of the lease, which didn't permit dogs, and so had to board him. That the Hardenberghs would have signed a lease for an apartment that didn't allow them to keep a dog is not quite in line with how they had always lived with him up to that point. The Hardenberghs had left Rags with friends on prior occasions when embarking on trips that were thought to have been too stressful for the terrier. On one of these occasions, Rags was hosted by friends on Long Island, who kept him (and he them) entertained an entire summer. What makes more sense, and is supported by statements made by both Richard Birney and Lieutenant Colonel Hardenbergh, is that as his condition worsened, Rags was brought to Aspin Hill because the Hardenberghs were simply unable to provide the level of care that the Birneys were qualified to offer.

The needs of a dog as old as Rags was are very complex. Just as humans do, dogs progress through stages where everyday functions taken for granted no longer conform to a timetable. Control is gradually lost, along with hearing and eyesight. The dog may live with pain from inflamed joints, decayed teeth, and internal organ dysfunction. There can be dementia, exacerbated by physical decline. As Rags grew deaf in his last years and the sight in his one good eye began to diminish until its light sputtered out, his world diminished along with his failing faculties.

For a dog in this condition, there was no better place to be than Aspin Hill. The *Montgomery Independent* reported in 1938 that the Birneys' business was considered exemplary and was recognized as "the only authorized animal hospital south of New York."[14] Richard Birney, who in later life was addressed with the title "Dr.," was not a veterinarian, but his reputation speaks for itself, and given his connections to animal lovers in Washington society, it is no surprise he was chosen to look after the ailing Rags. When the day came, the Hardenberghs wrapped the terrier in his blanket and drove him up to Aspin Hill, where he was accepted more as a patient than a boarder. In modern-day language, Rags was a palliative case, his symptoms managed because they could not be cured.[15]

Just as the circumstances of why Rags came to be at Aspin Hill are not exactly known, how long he lived after being brought there is also a mystery. However, we do know where at Aspin Hill he spent the last several weeks of his life. In an interview he gave two years after Rags's death, Birney told journalist John Patric that there was no way he would have boarded Rags in the kennels with all the other dogs. "I kept him in my home," he emphasized. Late winter and early spring in Maryland can be chilly, with cold, snowy days following deceptively sunny ones. Knowing how Rags had enjoyed sleeping under the Hardenberghs' kitchen stove, it is easy to imagine that he spent much of his time at the Birneys' home beside the stone fireplace in the living room, with its wide window letting in warm sun on bright days. We know from Birney that Rags was not the only dog occupying the house and that even at the end, Rags was as generous toward other dogs as he had been in his youth. "The old dog made friends with a puppy," Birney told Patric, "and wouldn't eat unless that pup had shared his dinner." So if Rags was blind, deaf, and in pain, at least nearby him were not only people caring for and loving him in his bewildered state but also a puppy who seems to have loved Rags, too.[16]

On March 19, 1936, using his Office of the Chief of Infantry letterhead, Raymond Hardenbergh wrote a letter to Capt. C. V. Allan of Second Corps Headquarters at Governors Island.

> Will you please, through G-2 office [army intelligence staff], endeavor to get in touch with one Jack Rohan. I believe he is or was at one time

connected with the M.I.D. Reserves [Military Intelligence Division]. He is a newspaper man and was employed by a press bureau in New York City but not the Associated Press.

Rohan is the author of a book called "Rags" and if you succeed in getting in touch with him I would like to have him know that Rags died about March 6th at the Aspin Hills Kennels near Rockville MD, and is buried in the dog cemetery in that place. Dr. Birney gave him every possible care during the last few months of his career. The old warrior passed out quietly from old age being at the time of his death, as nearly as I can figure it, between 18 and 19 years old.

I will be very grateful if you could convey this information to Jack Rohan and at the same time tell him that so far as I know the news of Rags' death has not appeared in any of the newspapers and that he is the first one in the newspaper field that I have told regarding Rags' death; also that I wanted him to have the information first for such use as he may wish to make of it.[17]

Hardenbergh added that he hoped Captain Allan could forward Rohan's address to him so he could communicate directly about the matter of setting up a memorial tablet to Rags. When Rohan's book first came out, First Division headquarters had agreed to manage Rags's share of royalties as a fund that would eventually pay for such a memorial at Fort Hamilton. Hardenbergh wished to discuss with Rohan whether the tablet shouldn't instead be placed on Rags's grave at Aspin Hill. (It is a moot point today, as the Hardenbergh descendants wish to leave Rags where he was interred.)[18]

Hardenbergh kept his word faithfully. Though less than a week after Rags's death the colonel received a letter from veteran New York journalist Minna Irving, asking for information about Rags for an article she was writing called "Mascots of the Service," he allowed even that venerable lady to remain in the dark for the time being.[19]

The day of Rags's burial, an officer—possibly Lieutenant Colonel Hardenbergh himself—placed a flag on the freshly upturned earth, a respectful gesture that would be repeated many times over the course of the year.[20]

Four days after Lieutenant Colonel Hardenbergh's letter was mailed, Jack Rohan sent off a response from his home on Staten Island:

Captain C. V. Allan, ADC to General Nolan has favored me with an extract from a letter which you sent to him announcing the passing of RAGS. I received it Saturday, the 21st, and feeling that the RAGS lovers in these parts should know of his death sent out a modest obituary.

Within ten minutes after the news hit the city desks of the newspapers the telephones began to ring—at my home, at the office of the Standard News Association and, I'm told the offices of the adjutants at Fort Hamilton and at Governors Island. They wanted details on Rags and plenty of them. I could scarcely trust my memory, no copy of the book was immediately available, so in most instances the newspapers relied on their own files. But Rags got considerably more space than did Prince [Serge] Mdvani [former brother-in-law of Woolworth heiress Barbara Hutton, killed in a Palm Beach polo match], who was being brought through New York for burial, or anyone else who died over the week-end, including John D. Rockefeller's personal physician [Dr. Harold E. Disbrow]. If you would care for them I shall be happy to send you such clippings as I am able to gather.[21]

As for the issue of whether, and where, to erect a tablet, Rohan went on to say:

There seems to be strong sentiment here, not only for erecting a memorial to RAGS, but for bringing his remains to Fort Hamilton and burying them there. General [Frank] Parker, I understand favors the idea. That of course is a matter entirely dependent on the wishes of the Hardenbergh family. Personally I hope you will agree to it. The memorial plans will of course involve expense considerably more than RAGS' personal "estate" [$52 at the time of writing] but that I suspect will increase considerably shortly. For the present I shall be glad to make a substantial personal contribution toward a memorial to him. It was, and is, my hope, that some day the old warrior's bequest to the "RAGS FUND" of the first division will run into substantial money. That has happened to books before. If the movies ever decide to produce the book the First Division certainly would have something to remember Rags by—and frankly so would I. However I am taking no hand in the memorial plans, will not until I hear from you. I merely announced that he had died, and certainly was surprised, not to say startled, at the reaction.[22]

Though like many members of the press then and now Rohan was prone to flights of exaggeration, he was by no means indulging in hyperbole when he described public response to Rags's death.

On March 22 there were few newspapers across America that did not print the terrier's obituary. The *Fresno Bee*, the *Salt Lake Tribune*, the *New York Post*, and the *New York Times* all published obituaries long and short, fanciful and true, based on Rohan's book or articles about Rags kept on file since the 1920s. The *Washington Post*'s obituary, one of the first to come out, made the front page and displayed a photo of Rags perched on a 75 mm gun and looking into the eyes of his buddy, Sergeant Hickman, whose account of his participation in Rags's rescue was included in the *New York Times* obituary a day later. Also quoted in the obituary was Maj. Gen. Frank Parker, commander of the First Division and one of the officers in the "generals with a dog" photo taken at the 1928 reunion. From Fort Hamilton, Parker said, "Since the beginning of history animals have shared the hardships of fighting men, and Rags was an outstanding example of devotion. He was a real soldier dog."[23]

Rags's death sent ripples across the national consciousness. When was a dog more than a dog? What did people owe a dog who had done for them everything that Rags had done? And what did society owe animals in general whose contribution of labor and food was taken almost entirely for granted? People weighed in from all sides.

One of the more touching letters the Hardenberghs received came from Kenji Onozawa, a Japanese American who had served for years as cook and servant for the family of Lt. Nicolas Campanole, friends of the Hardenberghs. Onozawa probably first met Rags in the kitchen of the Campanole home, where it can be imagined the terrier was given all the tidbits he wanted. "Please let me to express sorrow with you all," Onozawa wrote. "I heard over the Radio last night from [newsman and dog lover] Edwin C. Hill. Rag was good old dog and I want convey my regrets and we shall remember this day the most honored mascot of our Army."[24]

A New Yorker named R. Schnurmacher, who had never met Rags, was similarly stirred by news of his death. He wrote to the *New York Times*, "Now that the veterans have received their bonuses, how about a bonus for some of the dog heroes who served so valiantly and uncomplainingly during the World War?" Schnurmacher named Rags as well as a dog called Lieutenant Bobby, "the only dog officer in the army," then living in retirement in Jacksonville, Florida.[25] The writer added, "There were many others which served as dispatch bearers and mascots and dogs who were in later years trained to lead veterans blinded in the war. Surely they deserve some recognition from the government!"[26] Albert P. Terhune, owner of the famed Sunnybank collie kennels in Wayne, New Jersey, the dogs of which served as subject matter for his popular books, wrote in October, over six months after Rags had died, of the terrier's claim to two distinctions: as the best-known war dog in the world, one whose very existence "revived a thousand war memories in the minds of many thousand former service men," and also as one of the oldest dogs known anywhere.[27]

Minna Irving, alluded to earlier as having written to Lieutenant Colonel Hardenbergh about Rags just a few days after he died, did finally receive a reply.

Hardenbergh wrote her on March 31 that he appreciated her interest and hoped she would find in Jack Rohan's book and in the many articles in print since the news first broke on March 21 all the material she might need to include Rags in her "Mascots of Service" article. "If ever there was a mascot in the Service," Hardenbergh added, "he was certainly one."[28]

Irving did something better than just add Rags to the other mascots collected for her column. Among the Hardenbergh papers is a typed poem, still as creased as the day it was placed into an envelope and mailed. There is no record that it was published or indeed that it was composed for any but the eyes of Rags's family.

Brave Rags, the gallant dog of war
That at his master's side
Faced shot and shell, and gas and smoke
In battle's crimson tide
Has mustered out, and wearing still
The glory of his scars,
Has trotted up the shining road
That leads beyond the stars.
Play taps, and reel the muffled drums,
Half-mast the battle-flags,
A comrade of the AEF,
A hero true was Rags;
And in the peace of Paradise
A soldier as he waits,
Will hear an old familiar bark
And scratching at the gates,
And swing them wide to let him in
Where angels call the roll,
The loyal, loving mongrel dog,
The dog that had a soul.[29]

Shortly after Rags's burial, Lieutenant Colonel Hardenbergh wrote to Captain Allan at Governors Island that "the old dog certainly carried out his reputation for publicity until the end."[30] But aside from the flag left on his grave the day he was buried, Rags had had no funeral as such. That was about to change. On the now-grassy mound, visitors began to leave American flags. "A group of women come out here regularly," Birney noted, "and plant a fresh flag on the grave every time the old one becomes worn." These flags made Rags's grave as conspicuous as that of animals whose guardians had raised great slabs of marble to their memory.[31]

One day several months after Rags's burial, a short, stocky, middle-aged man paid a visit to Aspin Hill, saw Rags's flags twitching red, white, and blue in the sun, and went stomping back to his car.

Thurman Curtis Metcalf was a former commander of the Cissel-Saxon

THE DOG THAT HAD A SOUL

American Legion post at Silver Spring. Born in Virginia in 1896, Metcalf had registered for the draft in June 1918, a month before Rags was rescued in Paris, and was discharged in February 1919, around the time Donovan died at Fort Sheridan. Despite his age and size, Metcalf would register for World War II also—he was clearly as patriotic an American as one could find.[32] However, with a cruel irony, around the time of the first anniversary of Rags's death, Metcalf drafted and distributed a resolution through his former legion post that "the American flag was being desecrated by flying from the graves in Aspin Hill Cemetery," as a newspaper reported. The post commander felt it was his duty to forward the protest resolution all the way up to the Department of War, with "copies . . . sent to the Montgomery County Council of the legion and to DAR chapters."[33] Metcalf claimed that on his visit to Aspin Hill he had not only observed American flags planted on graves in an "improper and unpatriotic" manner but had also seen flags "thrown into a nearby gully with withered flowers and other refuse." As further evidence of desecration, Metcalf added that he had seen a flag on "the grave of a poodle named Skippy." In a sense, Metcalf's objections were old news where military mascots were concerned. After being given a nonmilitary medal in 1921 by Gen. John J. Pershing, "Yankee" Division mascot Sergeant Stubby was accused of having done "nothing, absolutely nothing, but sneak along behind his master and wonder what the hell was going on," wrote an infuriated correspondent to *Stars and Stripes* magazine. If the military saw fit to award medals to bull terriers, the writer went on, the next time there was a war, "send an army of bull pups" instead of "red-blooded American boys." As events were to bear out, however, these opinions were decidedly in the minority among the American public.[34]

When reporters came calling at Aspin Hill, they found a furious Richard Birney. A photograph in the *Washington Herald* shows him kneeling beside Rags's grave, which is studded not only with flags but with fresh flowers and even a Christmas wreath. His face is visibly stony with anger.

During an interview, he stood under the pines nearby, fairly spitting his words. He had not seen Metcalf's resolution, he said, but had already heard of its accusations. "I've heard a lot of things," he said, "but I never heard any such mess as this before. . . . I ask you if you see any desecration around here?" He reeled off Rags's military history, noting that on the day of his burial, the first flag was placed on his grave by an army officer, and other people had merely followed suit, with every honorable intention. "If they want to do something about this cemetery," he snapped, "why don't they help me raise some funds, as I've got a mind to do, to place a real monument on Rags' grave? But they never seem to come out here." As for acts of flag desecration on his property, he invited reporters to imagine what would happen if anybody had actually committed that crime: "Those good ladies who have their pets here would get behind it with shotguns." There wasn't even a gully for Metcalf to have seen any discarded flags in. Having blown his stack, Birney wanted no more of the conversation. "It was late in the afternoon when he left the cemetery to walk through a broomstraw field toward his house," reads the *Washington Post* article. "A half dozen or more fancy-bred dogs, which Birney boards, frisked about his heels, but he paid them no heed."[35]

As Maj. Edwin S. Bettelheim declared to the press at the time of the Aspin Hill uproar, during his service in France with the 104th Field Artillery, he and his men had buried their mascot dog, killed in action at Chemin des Dames (where Sergeant Stubby had first taken part in battle), wrapped in an American flag. At the time and after, no one thought to object. "A dog is man's best friend," said Bettelheim. "I can't see any desecration if the flag is used in the burial of man, dog or horse, so long as he served with honor."[36]

However, Thurman Metcalf's ability to whip up opposition among the members of his legion post showed that there were some retired military members who considered the integrity of a small cloth or paper rectangle set on a military dog's grave more important than the reason why the flag had been put there in the first place. Metcalf's attitude speaks to prejudices that do not die out over time. As dog writer Mary Elizabeth Thurston points out, after World War II undignified criticisms of medals of valor awarded to military dogs were not unknown among some members of the Veterans of Foreign Wars and the Order of the Purple Heart. "There's something about dogs being acknowledged as living, thinking beings that is really provocative to some people,"

Thurston says, "and military accolades are an easy target for such critics and speciesists. Of course, the burial of an animal as one would a human being, complete with graveside service, a headstone, flowers (or flags) has always pushed some people's buttons. They somehow think it equates the status of humans to that of 'lesser' beings, and to their minds that's a blasphemous thing."[37]

Most public response to Metcalf's allegations was swift, and many readers were outraged that anyone would deny a war hero the blessing of the flag on his grave, simply because he happened to be a dog.

Chief among the responses is a letter sent to a newspaper editor by a "True Patriot" and ex-serviceman. What was all the fuss about? asked the writer. "When will these pseudo patriots stop imbuing the flag with the ability to feel insults?" Though he had fought for it and lost his health for it in the trenches of France, the writer pointed out that the flag was merely "a piece of colored cloth," and as such an inanimate object. The flag was not a thing, it was a symbol, he insisted. The flag symbolized the freedom and security available to all Americans and to all whom America protected. It was for that freedom and security that he had fought in the Great War and would be willing to fight again if he had to. "This dog, yes, even a dog, is entitled to its protection," he wrote, "doubly so when he was willing to endanger his life for the flag's protection." Let the flag fly over Rags's grave, he insisted. Let it stand as a gesture of recognition, in honor of bravery, regardless of whether demonstrated by dog or human. "After all," the writer added in summation, "we can depend on a dog's faithfulness. Can the same be said of man?"[38]

12

War Hero

But when I found my poor old dog,
Though blind and deaf was he,
And feeble with his many years,
He turned and followed me.

—MINNA IRVING, "The Return" (1920)

Almost eighty years to the blustery March day when Rags had been buried there, I stood at his grave in Aspin Hill Memorial Park, watching a little American flag rise and fall in the breeze, thinking of the faithfulness of dogs.

A day earlier, I had driven to Maryland from Dartmouth College in Hanover, New Hampshire. The morning of my departure I was keen to get on my way for a long trip that would end at the Burtonsville home of Jay Butkus, grandson of Raymond and Helen Hardenbergh, and his wife, Judy, and their trove of Rags memorabilia. But I had something important to do before I hit the road. I had to see Alistair, the first and only canine mascot it had been my good fortune to meet.

On a prior visit to Dartmouth almost a decade before, I had become acquainted with a silky Cavalier King Charles spaniel who, at around two years of age, was already the reigning prince of the college's history department. With tennis ball as orb and rope as scepter, Alistair ruled the department lounge, offering his own form of student counseling via fetch and tug-of-war. He was even made the subject of a campus cartoon series, *The Many Moods of Alistair*, though he really only had one mood: that of amiable imp, his job in life not to disrupt human endeavor but to sweeten it. The one time his greeting to a couple of passersby was ignored, he was seen to stare quietly after them, his tail no longer wagging, as if pondering how he could have somehow failed in his mission to convert all humans to his combined faith of kindness and play.[1]

On that visit nine years ago, seated in a basket behind his guardian, Gail, Alistair had quickly sussed me out as the puppy pushover I am. Up he came, waddling in his fawn-and-white britches, and I'm happy to report he decided, after intense examination, that I was probably all right. We had quality time together on the office floor, and I remember thinking I should ask Gail to take a photo of us. But I was on a tight schedule, and I told Alistair before my departure, "We'll do it next time."

But that next time, almost ten years later, I entered Alistair's office and found him elderly, ill, and frail. He had nearly died twice, Gail told me, since I had last seen him. But he was still alert. When I spoke his name, Alistair came to me readily, eyes as bright as they were the first time, slowly but firmly snuggling my hand as he had done before. Again, on this trip, business had taken me away, which was why I hiked back to Carson Hall early next morning through snow that had blanketed the Green overnight. Shaking ice off my soles, I crouched down, Alistair beside me, so that Gail could capture us on my iPhone. Afterward, I told Alistair I would see him again. But as I got in my rental car and started the engine, my constricted throat and watering eyes told me this was not to be.

That is the chief beauty of a dog, I thought. It was a mantra I repeated as I drove south, dodging Connecticut snow squalls. No matter how long since last seen, no matter how much older each of us was, no matter anything, a dog will never forget you—just as Rags, despite the passing of time, encroaching age, and infirmities, recognized each of the survivors from the bloodbath of the Great War, though reunited with them in different surroundings so many years later. Like Alistair, like any dog, Rags never forgot a friend. Remembering Alistair's immediate, uncomplicated acknowledgment of me, I could understand something of what it had been like for the men of Governors Island, Fort Hancock, and Fort Hamilton when the mascot many half-remembered and others thought was dead came running up to them as if years were nothing, as if the trauma and comedy of war had only happened yesterday.

Shortly after starting my drive to Maryland, I realized I was on a reverse course from the one Rags had taken on his 1929 stowaway truck ride from Washington DC to Governors Island, and it felt as if he had hitched passage south with me in my little white rental. Crossing the George Washington Bridge to the flat freeways of New Jersey, Rags and I looked over at a New York skyline not terribly different, aside from the looming Freedom Tower, from the one he'd known on Governors Island in the twenties and thirties. Approaching Trenton, I wondered if somewhere nearby was the place on the side of the road where the Governors Island truck drivers had stopped on discovering their canine hitchhiker, where they fed Rags their rations for breakfast, just like the old battlefield days in France. Skirting or crossing rivers from New York to Maryland, I imagined Rags thrusting his muzzle out my passenger window, as he had no doubt done over the edge of the truck bed, to sample the local aromas.

Even after I was met at their front door by Judy and Jay Butkus, who live about ten miles from Aspin Hill, I felt as if I had not stopped moving, as if Rags was still with me in this house that held such tangible evidence of his history.

The Butkuses and I recognized each other immediately, because our shared love of animals made us family.

All sorts of objects in the Butkus house reminded me of their love of animals. A glowing pastel portrait of Helen Wolcott Stewart Johnson, future wife of Lt. Raymond Waite Hardenbergh, brought to mind her many dogs, one of which, Jock, had worn a special silver collar that is still kept polished and on display a century later, as if waiting for Jock to return and wear it.

"And this is what we call the Rags Corner," Judy told me. On the wall were framed photos of Rags along with clippings celebrating his high points as First Division mascot. There was an even more tangible reminder of the terrier. Judy put something in my hand. "Do you know whose this was?" she teased. I looked down at a rectangle of black leather dried with age, about an inch and a half wide by two and a half inches in length. Riveted in its center was a metal plate, engraved. It read, "VV Rags V 1st Div. A.E.F. Maj. Hardenbergh U.S. Army." This was the tag that, first seen by soldiers at Governors Island in 1925, had brought Rags back into the limelight as mascot of the First Division, the tag that the policemen puzzled over in Washington but that General Pershing did not need to see, knowing exactly who the half-blinded, limping, and coughing little hero was.

Judy and I settled on a sofa to look at family photo albums, on each thick black page of which Rags jumped or sprawled, barked or lazed in a variety of settings. There were pictures of Sue Hardenbergh, Jay's mother, with Rags (Sue had married Lt. Col. Dr. Walter Anthony Butkus), of Rags having his head ruffled by smiling girlfriends of the Hardenbergh sisters, of Rags stretching out on parade ground grass, of Rags sitting in the rumble seat of a Model-T Ford, captured in the very upright posture of an elderly passenger unsure of what to expect next.

"This may sound strange," Judy began, as we leafed through the album. She is a retired teacher, with a lilt of Virginia in her voice and a smile like sunshine. Nothing she says would seem strange to me, but I asked her to go on. "Sometimes," Judy said, "it feels as if Rags is still here." That *was* strange, but not the way Judy seemed to think I would take it to be. When I'd first entered the Butkus home, I was surprised to find that though the house had all the earmarks of dog occupancy, or rather the feel of it, no dogs were present, at least not in the corporeal sense. It was not just the wall of Rags photographs and clippings or his collar tag on display. It was something intangible but real, as if the love shared by this dog and his people had taken on a separate, immortal life of its own.

Next morning, on our drive to Aspin Hill, Jay, Judy, and I stopped to pick up another family member.

Helen Seitz is the widow of John F. R. Seitz, son of Helen Hardenbergh and Maj. Gen. John Seitz.[2] Helen is elegant, direct, and intensely curious; we hit it off immediately. I found out that she and her late husband had had a marker placed on Rags's grave in 1991. They felt they needed to do something about Rags's bare plot when, on finding there was a space beside his, they used it for burial of their beloved dog Fonzi.

"We went into the old house to look at the burial register," Helen told me. "That was how we confirmed where Rags was and where Fonzi could go." She added, "We wanted to put up a more impressive monument for Rags, but it wasn't offered. Either the upright stone or one flat on the ground. We chose the upright one for both."

Helen didn't know why the United States Army had never followed through on what were clearly serious intentions of commissioning a memorial tablet to Rags either at Aspin Hill or at Fort Hamilton. The parlous state of the U.S. economy in 1936 and the worse state of its military's finances are likely why nothing ever happened. Perhaps the $52 in book royalties Rags was said to have left at his death was not enough to pay for what the officers had in mind. And though Jack Rohan had promised Major Hardenbergh that he would donate a considerable amount of his own cash to the memorial fund, this promise was made in the middle of the Depression. If he had had to renege, who could blame him? Apart from anything else, a little over a year after Rags died another world war would slowly explode across Europe. And so memories of Rags faded. Given that he wasn't stuffed and displayed in a museum, like Sergeant Stubby, it was a case of out of sight, out of mind.

En route to the cemetery, we stopped once more to fetch a friend who knew a great deal about the history of Aspin Hill.

b j Altschul met me at the door of her house—"the only pink Colonial on the street; can't miss it"—and with her was her beagle, Cori, whom b j had adopted from the Montgomery County Humane Society, owner of Aspin Hill. b j had served as director of external relations for the MCHS until health problems made it necessary to resign.

I was intrigued to find that b j and I had both been hooked by Diane Beers's book *For the Prevention of Cruelty*. As b j wrote in 2006 in her blog, *Web of Life*, the book had moved her "to translate good intentions into actions where humane activism is concerned."[3] A year before we met, b j was interviewed at Aspin Hill. Just like Richard Birney, b j said that with adequate funding, Aspin Hill could become an educational center for animal welfare, a place to show children the importance of care and compassion. "This is something," b j told the newsman, looking around her, "that will really allow us to shine a spotlight on what humane living can be."[4]

During my research for this book, and despite her worsening health, b j had discovered and shared with me dozens of newspaper articles dealing with Aspin Hill. By the time plans were afoot to visit Rags's grave, she was very fragile, but she insisted on joining us. And as Jay navigated traffic, b j described for us everything she knew of Aspin Hill's past, from documented fact to scurrilous scuttlebutt.

In 1946 the Birneys sold Aspin Hill to a Dr. Edgar Reubush, a veterinarian, who sold it fifteen years later to S. Alfred Nash, an embalmer. Until 1987 Aspin Hill was relatively quiet. Then in 1988 all hell broke loose, making the flag controversy look like a walk in the park.

That year, a developer bid on the eight-acre property, his plan to level the site for an office condominium complex. Instead of the apathy he may have expected, the developer touched off a war among local residents as well as people whose animal and human family were buried at Aspin Hill. As B. P. Robert Stephen Silverman wrote, "The Battle of Aspin Hill is one of the most inspiring love stories of all time."[5] The main sticking point was that nobody had ever drawn up a covenant restricting what could be done to alter the property. But that was to change, surprising even those who fought for it. "Enormous political pressure from the plot holders culminated in an upset victory," wrote Silverman, whose dogs are buried on the site.[6] The Montgomery County Council refused to approve the bid. Then came a kind-hearted philanthropist, who purchased the property to prevent this kind of crisis happening again.

The fairy godmother who saved Rags's and the other animals' final resting place was Dorothy Shapiro. Born in Portland, Oregon, in 1921, Dorothy married Maurice Shapiro, whose real estate development business made them a fortune they used to help a wide variety of causes and institutions, including George Washington University, the United States Holocaust Museum, and national and local animal welfare programs. Described in her *Washington Post* obituary as "small, wiry and white-haired," Dorothy was no airy heiress with lady's maids and poodles. "She pretended to be an ordinary little old lady. She was a free spirit who indulged in swing dancing into her eighties. She also loved animals. Her Potomac home was full of dogs and cats, her back yard peopled with deer, opossums, raccoons, foxes, geese and any four-legged or two-legged feathered or furry friend that came by," described Dorothy's personal assistant, Annaliese Mudrak.[7]

Aspin Hill was acreage intensely close to Dorothy's heart: some thirty of her and Maurice's pet dogs are interred there. She laid out $400,000 to buy Aspin Hill. Having assured the property's security, she had the necessary covenants drawn up and spent another six figures of her money on the site's future maintenance.

By 1992 Aspin Hill was described as "an ark in the suburbs," and that it was, quite literally. Dorothy Shapiro had turned the property over to People for the Ethical Treatment of Animals (PETA). Cofounder and national director Ingrid Newkirk, to some a visionary warrior for animal welfare, to others a "combative, sharp-tongued, media-manipulating" fanatic, lived in the Birney house for a period of time. "When PETA was given the property," Newkirk says, "it was in total disrepair and with the cemetery completely overgrown so that the gravesites could not be seen, perhaps the tops in some places. I supervised the interns until we could find a 'house mother,' and worked with weekend crews cleaning up the grounds, removing weeds, making the place visitable and presentable again."[8]

"The dining room, den and breakfast nook have been converted to a giant, floor-to-ceiling birdhouse for abused birds," wrote journalist Mary Pemberton in 1993. Among these were a white cockatoo rescued by singer-songwriter James Taylor, sixty parakeets saved from an attic, and a truly tragic case, a cockatoo with wings severed for use as a decoy to trap other birds for the exotic pet market. Newkirk originally had big plans for Aspin Hill. The sanctuary was to become an education center for schoolchildren. PETA erected monuments in memory of animals killed for the fur industry and in scientific experiments, and a marker was laid down in memory of Mickey, a Doberman pinscher seized in an abuse case. Newkirk also made Aspin Hill a destination for celebrities supportive of animal welfare. "PETA added a gloss of glamour," wrote Cameron W. Barr for the *Washington Post*.[9] It was during these years that Rags's grave received its granite marker, and his presence there and his history as a military mascot were rediscovered and honored.[10]

By the mid-1990s, PETA's offices had moved from Maryland to Virginia, so Dorothy Shapiro shopped around for another manager and found Dianne D. Pearce, director of the Chesapeake Wildlife Sanctuary. Dorothy was extremely choosy about how her gifts were to be used.[11] And at first, all went as she expected and as Pearce had promised. Then complaints began to arise about how the property looked. "People are questioning why the historic Aspin Hill Pet Cemetery is taking on the look of a marina," stated a Gaithersburg journalist. More than a dozen vehicles were parked all over the property, including "at least eight boats." For Dorothy Shapiro, there were darker concerns. The Charities and Legal Services Division of Maryland began drilling down into Pearce's management at Aspin Hill, and she was judged "increasingly delinquent in filing annual reports and disclosure statements."[12]

In June 2005 Dorothy filed suit against Pearce.[13] Almost two years later, a Montgomery County Circuit Court judge awarded the property back to Shapiro, who conveyed it to the Montgomery County Humane Society the following month and began to clean the site.[14]

The 2008 recession hit the MCHS hard; they couldn't cover basic grounds-keeping expenses at Aspin Hill. As the Birney house and outbuildings continued to decay, Montgomery County condemned the property. "The humane society sought, and the county granted, an extension that gives the group until March 2010 to make repairs or face demolition of buildings, including a house, which date to about 1921," wrote Margie Hyslop of the *Gazette*. The MCHS couldn't even sell plots for profit because nobody knew who was buried where. The burial register that Helen Seitz consulted in 1991 had vanished.[15]

Matters had improved by 2010; volunteers stood up to help, and the cemetery was put in order, but Dorothy Shapiro was not happy with the way the property looked. By 2011 the MCHS had succeeded in lobbying the Montgomery County Planning Board to approve a zoning change, needed for the society to open offices in the Birney house and restore the cemetery, preparing it for business and tours once again. They also explored adding an animal clinic and animal welfare classes to generate revenue. MCHS president and CEO Cris Bombaugh promised Shapiro that the organization would do everything exactly as she wished. Even so, when Dorothy died in June 2012, many of her and the Humane Society's challenges remained in need of solutions.[16]

As we approached the gentle knoll of Aspin Hill, b j said, "We still desperately need volunteers. We are grateful for the one-time visits, but the upkeep continues to be a need all year round. Storms bring down branches in the spring, the grass grows tall in the summer. It needs cutting again and again until winter. Sometimes people who visit the cemetery can't walk through it because of the vegetation. We are working on this and on a plan for the entire park. But we need community buy-in to succeed." And money, she added. Always money.

Jay parked inside the property, and we stepped out of the car. A first glance revealed why some plot owners, especially the elderly, might decide they valued their ankles, knees, or neck more than braving stray branches and overgrown shrubs to visit the grave of their pet. I could also see why volunteers might not return regularly every week or month, though ideally that is what needed to happen at Aspin Hill. I had seen photographs of Aspin Hill from the 1920s, and I knew what park-like beauty it was capable of. Like all beauty, it comes at the high price of unstinting upkeep; it needs the eyes and hands of those whose care doesn't have a shelf life or a season.

Despite these disturbingly visible realities of a property with the appearance of living on borrowed time, the effect was quite the opposite of sad. Granite and marble, hard, unforgiving surfaces, bore such tender, endearing names: Tinsel, Toodles, Baby, Poochie (whose enameled photograph, many decades old, shows a bright-eyed black Pomeranian). Tender and endearing, too, are the messages inscribed on these stones. "In memory of Snookums: A True Friend and Faithful Pal," states one slab. "Lovely soul, he lives on / And in that sweet bye and bye / We shall meet again on that beautiful shore," sings another.

With human gravestones, even carved by a naive chisel, death's heads seem to speak of the grave as unavoidable penance for merely having lived. For the animals of Aspin Hill, the grave was a place of sweet sleep for innocents gone too soon, none in danger of a next world bitter with regrets for earthly sins.

Some would argue that the money spent on such markers would have been better off donated to rescue and care for living animals, thousands of which are in need of homes. I can appreciate that. But for me, the fact that the people whose pets these had been had gone to such trouble, in some cases such sacrifice, to commemorate a member of their animal family in such a beautiful setting among so many other beloved animals stood as Aspin Hill's chiefest defense. Rags, Mickey, Tinsel, the horses and cats, birds and rabbits, and the monkey, Andy, who had spent her short, busy life helping her homeless guardian collect coins on street corners, were long dead. But though the brevity of their lives could never be fully mourned (and we know only half their story, being shut out from an animal's inner world), the love they inspired was celebrated in indestructible stone and in memory, that nebulous thing that lasts even longer.

"So we turn left at Mickey's mausoleum," explained Helen as she guided us through the grounds. "Turn, and you'll see Rags and Fonzi."

From Mickey's tomb, I looked as directed, and there I saw it. Down a path bordered by other stones, the lives and loves of other people's dogs, were the gray granite markers special to our group. One of them was the grave of Fonzi; beside his stone stood another: "Rags—War Hero—1st Division Mascot—WWI—1916-1936." Judy leaned down with bouquets of orange alstroemeria and tulips tied with ribbon, a bunch for each dog. Dry leaves tossed in a cold wind.

As we stood there, each in our own spinning emotional world, I thought back to newspaper clippings I had seen of Richard Birney kneeling beside this grave, straightening its flags during the Metcalf controversy. There should be flags here now, and I kicked myself for not having thought to bring one with me. And this thought, in turn, reminded me of what Birney had told John Patric in 1938. Birney had said he kept Rags in his house, and it was there Rags had died in his sleep—the house that, until recently, had been under threat of demolition by the county. I glanced around, but Helen had already read my mind. "It's still there," she said softly, pointing beyond the trees and bushes.

Judy and Helen came with me. We stopped at the wire fence that separated the house from the cemetery. I stood there, looking at the red-brick cottage, mentally calculating what I might need to do in order to get closer to it—perhaps find a window in the living room that was not covered through which I might see the fireplace where Rags slept his last in March 1936. When Judy and Helen walked back to the car, I continued to stand for as long as I could without inconveniencing our lunch plans.

That's when I saw it. Down near the weed-choked tangle at the base of the fence lay a small American flag. It was made of cloth, and together with its gold-painted finial it appeared as if it had never been exposed to weather. I picked it up and looked around to see where such a flag could conceivably have come from. On a breezy day like this, it could easily have blown against the fence from off one of the graves. Yet though I searched, I couldn't find any plots close enough for the flag to have been planted there. And then it dawned on me. I walked back to the group, waving the flag. "Can you believe what I just found?" I asked them. "Shall I give it to Rags?" I saw Judy's eyes brim, saw Helen smile in firm approval. Back I went, turning left at Mickey's mausoleum. Kneeling on the dry leaves, I pushed the flag into the hard earth beside Rags's marker.

I had started my journey to this spot the same day Rags had died seventy-eight years earlier, and here I was, a few days away from the anniversary of his burial, planting a flag as others had done.

As a supporter of animal welfare, I can never read of animals in warfare without a stab to the heart and an echo of the words inscribed on the Animals in War monument in London: "They had no choice." Yet standing there, watching the breeze lift Rags's flag to meet sunshine that suddenly, startlingly, streamed down, I realized that his rescue had been just that.

When Jimmy Donovan, George Hickman, and the other soldiers of the First Division had taken Rags into their human world of war, they had given him a new and wonderful life. It was one perhaps no less dangerous than the hardscrabble existence of an unwanted street stray, but it was a life that, while never safe, not even after he arrived in America, had nonetheless given Rags a purpose, a role to fill. He had found somebody who wanted him. When he followed two American soldiers exiting a Montmartre café that Bastille Day in 1918, Rags rescued himself.

NOTES

PROLOGUE

1. "Dog Hero Balks at 'Finger' Printing," *New York Times*, undated clipping, Butkus Collection.
2. H. I. Phillips, "The Once Over," undated clipping, Butkus Collection.
3. Minna Irving (Minnie Odell Michiner, 1857-1940), undated typescript, Butkus Collection. Irving's poem has much in common with "The Curate Thinks You Have No Soul," a poem about the death of a dog by St. John Lucas (1879-1934), which was carved on the gravestone of a collie at Aspin Hill Memorial Park, Silver Spring, Maryland.
4. "Army Enters 'Rags' in Popularity Contest," *New York Times*, November 4, 1926.
5. Gabriel Boissy quoted in Le Naour, *The Living Unknown Soldier*, 76.
6. "Rags, Dog Veteran of War, Is Dead at 20; Terrier That Lost Eye in Service Is Honored," *New York Times*, March 22, 1936.
7. For information about Nowzad, see http://www.nowzad.com/.
8. Rohan, *Rags*, 242; Goodavage, *Soldier Dogs*, 13.

1. THE HILL OF MARS

1. Peter Allen, "French Built Replica Paris after First World War to Fool German Bombers," *Daily Mail*, November 10, 2011.
2. Young, "Archaeology in an Urban Setting."
3. Young, "Archaeology in an Urban Setting."
4. See Coolidge on the bomb that landed near the Gare du Nord and on the particularly cold Parisian winter and spring of 1917 (*A War Diary*, 253, 198-220). Don, the collie-mix mascot of Company B, 106th Infantry, was accustomed to exploding shells, but when a bomb landed too close to him, he went absent without leave in June 1918. He found his way back to his trench two days later, and the experience evidently cured him of fear, as he was wounded at Vierstraat Ridge and on the Hindenburg Line in the fall of 1918, returning to New York City with the surviving members of the company in March 1919. Also see "Lynbrook Dog Won Fame."
5. Link, "The Enigma," 308.

NOTES TO PAGES 8–15

6. On xenophobia, see "The War and German Americans," http://www.learnnc
.org/lp/editions/nchist-newcentury/5764, 2009; the text quote is from "T.R.
Talks at Plattsburg," *New York Times*, August 26, 1915.

7. Nelson, *Five Lieutenants*, 7–10.

8. Mead, *The Doughboys*, 135.

9. Pershing, *My Experiences*, 91–93.

10. Mead, *The Doughboys*, 112–13.

11. *American Legion Weekly*, September 5, 1924.

12. Bausum, *Sergeant Stubby*, 167–69; for the Putnam/Peking story, see "The
Army Pensions Faithful Gun Horse," *New York Times*, November 8, 1908.
During the war, General Pershing made time to send his thanks in a letter
to the American Red Star, an animal-oriented Red Cross formed by the
American Humane Association in 1916, for their assistance in the care of
animals injured in the Great war. See Beers, *For the Prevention of Cruelty*,
100–101.

13. Pershing, *My Experiences*, 93.

2. A DOG'S LIFE

1. 1920 United States Census; 1918 draft card (Family History Library roll no.
1613406). According to the 1953 Manhattan City Directory, Jack Rohan was
still living at 40 East 10th in Greenwich Village. He died ten years later.
Census, draft card, and Manhattan city directory data available through
Ancestry.com.

2. Text from Jack Rohan's Samuel Colt biography (New York: Harper & Brothers,
1935), dust jacket author blurb. There is at least more proof of Rohan's career
at this point in his life than for another of his claims: that after retiring from
active service, he "served for a time as advisor to the Minister of Information
in Greece." Rohan also claimed to have written a history of the United States
armed forces, published serially, but it does not appear among his known
works cataloged in the Library of Congress. In a letter dated March 1936
written to the aide-de-camp of Gen. Dennis E. Nolan, Lt. Col. Raymond W.
Hardenbergh refers to Rohan's past connection with the MID Reserves, the
Military Intelligence Division.

3. Susan Hardenbergh, daughter of Maj. Raymond W. Hardenbergh, told a
family member she did not care for some of the embellishments Rohan
introduced into Rags's life story. Helen Seitz to author, March 14, 2014.

4. "Donovan's captain . . . was desertion": Rohan, *Rags*, 1; "In hope of finding
a star . . . soft and yielding": Rohan, *Rags*, 2; "Rags, sir": Rohan, *Rags*, 6. The
name "Rags" must have been a popular one for scruffy dogs. In 1916, the
year Rags was said to have been born in Paris, Duckworth & Company in
London published *Rags: The Diary of a Dog of War*, with text and illustrations

by Ernest Noble. The forty-seven-page book purports to be the diary of a small wire-haired terrier (often shown wearing his master's regimental Glengarry) named Rags whose master went off to war in France. Rags goes to the battlefields of France to find him and has adventures along the way. In 2014 author Margot Theis Raven published *Rags: Hero Dog of WWI* (Ann Arbor, MI: Sleeping Bear Press), a version of Rags's and Donovan's story for children with illustrations by Petra Brown. Shortly after the book's publication, in August, the centenary of the start of the Great War, Raven died after a long battle with cancer. Writing about Rags and Rags's own bravery, Raven's husband told me, had kept her going till the book was finished.

5. "Rags, Dog Veteran of War." In 2014, as this book was being completed, M.Sgt. R. L. Baker of the U.S. Army Military History Institute in Carlisle, Pennsylvania, performed a search for any trace of James Donovan, as private and as a member of the signal corps, and found nothing in the postwar unit histories on the Seventh Field Artillery and the First Infantry Division. That "Jimmy" (possibly a nickname) existed is attested to by the fact that when Rags was entered in a dog show in 1925, the men at Governors Island created a placard telling the history of Rags and Donovan that was displayed in public then and for several years afterward. Had Donovan been a pseudonym or his history been made up altogether, it hardly follows that officers like Charles P. Summerall, Lucius R. Holbrook, and Hugh A. Drum, who had known Rags in the field in France, would pose with Rags in front of this placard or associate themselves with a story based on a fictitious soldier, especially when so many who had died carrying out brave missions were unknown to and uncelebrated by the general public. A few years before Rags's "rediscovery" on Governors Island, while living at Fort Sheridan, Mrs. Helen Hardenbergh was aware that the young soldier whom Rags was attached to was named Donovan, as borne out in an interview she gave shortly afterward. As I speculate in this book, the Hardenberghs may well have arrived at Fort Sheridan before Donovan's death, because they met Rags when he was spending time at the base hospital, where Donovan was a patient, and Rags was described as never going near the building after Donovan's death. The likely destruction of Donovan's war records in the 1973 fire at the National Personnel Records Center complicates the case— 80 percent of army records, of which no copies or indexes were kept, were lost. See "The National Personnel Records Center (NPRC) Fire: A Study in Disaster," http://www.archives.gov/st-louis/military-personnel/fire-1973.html.

6. "Rags in a Dog Show; Has a War Record," *New York Times*, October 9, 1925; "Family Tree Bars Army Dog at Show," *New York Times*, October 10, 1925.

7. George Hickman to Mrs. J. F. Wilson, July 28, 1918, and Hickman's *feuille de route* (marching orders) for June 22, 1918, Kemmerer Collection; Jaffin, "Medical Support," 107–8.

8. George Hickman to Mrs. J. F. Wilson, July 28, 1918, Kemmerer Collection.
9. One of the most famous mascots in military history was Boy, a white poodle who belonged to Prince Rupert of the Rhine. Boy fulfilled this definition and was believed to bring fine fortune not just to the prince during the English Civil War but to the royalist side of the conflict. Predictably, Roundheads were not Boy's fans, considering him a "Popish, profane Dog, more than halfe a divell." Magic charm he may have been, but Boy died for love. When the prince neglected to tie him securely behind the lines, Boy followed the commander into the field, where his coat made him an easy target for Roundhead bullets. MacDonogh, *Reigning Cats and Dogs*, 208–9.
10. Baynes, *Animal Heroes*, 7, 9–10.
11. "Lynbrook Dog Won Fame in Army."
12. Baynes and Fuentes, *Book of Dogs*, 17.
13. Rohan, *Rags*, 9–10, 17.

3. WAR DOG

1. "From Pet to Hero," 2015, http://soldierdog.net/messenger-dogs.
2. Cooper, *Animals in War*, 81.
3. Richardson, *British War Dogs*, 117–18.
4. Richardson, *British War Dogs*, 122–23.
5. Richardson, *British War Dogs*, 119. In *Soldier Dogs* (56–61), Goodavage writes of an explosive detector dog (EDD) named Lars J274, a cheeky Jack Russell terrier who was meant to be trained as a drug detection dog but became an EDD by accident. He was put to work for the United States Navy, which uses Jack Russells, perfect by size and persistence, to squeeze into small spaces sniffing for hidden explosives.
6. Quoted in Lengel, *To Conquer Hell*, 74–75.
7. Rohan, *Rags*, 15–17, 22.
8. Van Emden, *Tommy's Ark*, 146.
9. United States Army, Seventh Field Artillery Regiment, *History*, 66–67, 68.
10. Francis and Austin quoted in Mead, *The Doughboys*, 258, 259.
11. Rohan, *Rags*, 18.

4. A MATCH MADE IN HELL

1. Gillespie and Ewart quoted in van Emden, *Tommy's Ark*, 77–78, 164.
2. Smythe quoted in Masson, *Dogs Never Lie*, 105.
3. For army regulations on mascots, see Lemish, *War Dogs*, 24–25.
4. Lemish, *War Dogs*, 20, quoting Richardson.
5. Richardson, *British War Dogs*, 65.
6. The connection between Rags and Donovan was described by modern-day soldier Spc. Joel Eugenides, who had an "incredibly close" bond with his

Specialized Search Dog (SSD), Laila, who served with him in Afghanistan in 2009–10 and today lives with him and his family as an Emotional Support Animal. "You wind up picking up on little body language cues," says Eugenides, "that you wouldn't even be able to tell existed unless you had worked with each other so closely for so long. . . . We definitely had a relationship no one could truly understand without having had [an SSD] themselves at one point." It wasn't long, Eugenides adds, before he and Laila were communicating, "just from a simple look. . . . She is the only dog I will have ever trusted my life with." Brought together by training, in the field of action Eugenides and Laila found a deeper bond. Joel Eugenides to author, September 26, 2014.

7. Rohan, *Rags*, 19–20.

8. Richardson, *British War Dogs*, 68.

9. Ellis, *Eye-Deep in Hell*, 17.

10. Rohan, *Rags*, 21–22. Welch is not listed in the First Division's Roll of Honor; not all casualties were, particularly gas casualties. This may account for why Donovan is not listed.

11. Liz Whitlock, "Dogs of Modern War, Part 2: WWI." *Wilmington Examiner*, May 27, 2013, http://www.examiner.com/article/dogs-of-modern-war -part-2-world-war-i.

12. Orsi, "Effectiveness," 62. Not many runners lived till the end of an offensive or emerged from the war unwounded. Among the lucky ones was Six Nations Onondaga athlete Tom Charles Longboat, who ran dispatches for the Canadian 107th Pioneer Battalion, was wounded, and once even was left for dead. Though he served bravely, Longboat never received a citation for his work—in common with other survivors of this dangerous, vital, but easily dismissed war service.

13. Rohan, *Rags*, 23.

14. Thomas quoted in Clark, *The American Expeditionary Force*, 36.

15. Regimental Adjutant, Twenty-Sixth Infantry, *The Twenty-Sixth Infantry in France*, 27.

16. Ellis, *Eye-Deep in Hell*, 10.

17. United States Army, Seventh Field Artillery Regiment, *History*, 79.

18. Summerall, *The Way of Duty*, 133.

19. Rohan, *Rags*, 26.

20. Rohan, *Rags*, 56; Orsi, "Effectiveness," 37.

21. Rohan, *Rags*, 36.

22. Rohan, *Rags*, 41–42; Baynes, *Animal Heroes*, 7.

23. Rohan, *Rags*, 46–47.

24. Summerall, *The Way of Duty*, 50.

25. Rohan, *Rags*, 29–30.

26. Rohan, *Rags*, 54.

5. LAST BATTLE

1. Marshall, *Memoirs of My Services,* 137. The German *Stellungen,* or lines (Kriem-hild Stellung, Giselher Stellung, Hagen Stellung, etc.), were not named for "witches" in the operas of Richard Wagner, as some authors have written, but for legendary Norse heroes co-opted first by German nationalist mytho-poesis, later by the composer himself, and later still as part of the mythology of German imperial power, down to the time of Adolf Hitler.
2. Lengel, *To Conquer Hell,* 71.
3. Marshall, *Memoirs of My Services,* 154.
4. United States Army, Seventh Field Artillery Regiment, *History,* 96.
5. Orsi, "Effectiveness," 76.
6. Gillespie quoted in van Emden, *Tommy's Ark,* 74.
7. United States Army, Seventh Field Artillery Regiment, *History,* 96.
8. Rohan, *Rags,* 67.
9. Barnwell Rhett Legge (1891–1949), later brigadier general, served as mili-tary attaché to Switzerland during World War II. Legge was awarded the Distinguished Service Cross for his performance during the Battle of the Meuse-Argonne. Capt. Shipley Thomas (b. 1892, alive in 1972) wrote a his-tory of the American Expeditionary Forces, published in 1920.
10. Rohan, *Rags,* 57.
11. Regimental Adjutant, Twenty-Sixth Infantry, *The Twenty-Sixth Infantry in France,* 45.
12. Cochrane, *Gas Warfare,* 28.
13. Rohan, *Rags,* 68.
14. Rohan, *Rags,* 68; Cochrane, *Gas Warfare,* 28; Regimental Adjutant, Twenty-Sixth Infantry, *The Twenty-Sixth Infantry in France,* 45.
15. United States Army, Seventh Field Artillery Regiment, *History,* 45.
16. Orsi, "Effectiveness," 81.
17. Rohan, *Rags,* 71; Marshall, *Memoirs of My Services,* 135.
18. Cochrane, *Gas Warfare,* 41.
19. Regimental Adjutant, Twenty-Sixth Infantry, *The Twenty-Sixth Infantry in France,* 46.
20. Rohan, *Rags,* 72–73.
21. Chaney quoted in van Emden, *Tommy's Ark,* 262.
22. "'Sergeant Rags' a Yellow-Haired Mut[sic]," *Indiana Evening Gazette,* June 9, 1926.
23. Rohan, *Rags,* 73.
24. Rohan, *Rags,* 74; *Stars and Stripes,* November 8, 1954, 8.
25. Rohan, *Rags,* 74–76.
26. Rohan, *Rags,* 76; Holbrook information: *Stars and Stripes,* November 8, 1954, 8.
27. Rohan, *Rags,* 78.

28. Rohan, *Rags*, 79.

29. Rohan, *Rags*, 80–81.

30. Rohan, *Rags*, 82, 83.

31. Rohan, *Rags*, 83.

32. Rohan, *Rags*, 87–89.

33. Cochrane, *Gas Warfare*, 39–40.

34. Rohan, *Rags*, 90.

35. Rohan, *Rags*, 91.

36. Rohan, *Rags*, 91–92.

37. Cooper, in *Animals in War* (65), touches on the story of Dorothy Brooke, an English general's wife living in Cairo who in 1930 was horrified to find surviving British war horses, mules, and donkeys laboring, though skin and bones, in the streets of the city and in stone quarries nearby. Perhaps most heartbreaking of all, as Brooke pointed out, was the way these emaciated, overworked horses pricked up their ears at the sound of her English voice. Brooke purchased as many as she could and later founded The Brooke, a sanctuary now spread across several nations, where the organization focuses not just on equine welfare (provided free of charge) but on educating the people living in these societies in the responsibilities involved in caring for beasts of burden.

38. Halstead Dorey memorial, West Point Association of Graduates. http://apps .westpointaog.org/Memorials/Article/3784/.

39. Rohan, *Rags*, 92.

40. Rohan, *Rags*, 97.

41. "World War I Mascot; 18th Infantry Scrapbook Holds Dog's Obituary," *Stars and Stripes*, November 8, 1948.

42. Rohan, *Rags*, 95–96.

6. NEW WORLD

1. Rohan, *Rags*, 101.

2. Rohan, *Rags*, 101.

3. Rohan, *Rags*, 102.

4. Army School of Nursing, Class of 1921, *The Annual*, 225.

5. Rhett, *The History of Fort Sheridan*, 44.

6. Rhett, *The History of Fort Sheridan*, 46.

7. Rohan, *Rags*, 103. In 2014, when this book was close to being completed, a dog in the Dongbei region of northeastern China showed extraordinary loyalty toward its hospitalized master. According to a news report posted by DuoDuo Animal Welfare Project, a California-based charity supporting the need for improved animal welfare in China and Taiwan, the small black-and-tan mixed breed followed its owner into the hospital, trying to get on the gurney. It then waited for hours outside the emergency room door.

8. I believe this best approximates the chronology. From the time of Donovan's hospitalization in October 1918, Rohan places him successively in a dressing station, then a field hospital, and then the monastery hospital (the last two for some weeks), then has him sailing on the hospital ship, and finally the train trip to Fort Sheridan. All of this must logically more than exceed a month and perhaps much more. Given this scenario, we would expect Donovan to have arrived at Fort Sheridan no later than sometime in early December 1918. As his records are missing, we don't know when he died, but I presume this took place in early 1919. However, his death could have taken place later. Rohan's account and testimony given by the Hardenbergh family in interviews later on indicate they first encountered Rags at Fort Sheridan in 1920, where they met him "at the hospital." Since Rohan insists that Rags never went near the hospital again after Donovan died, this suggests that Donovan was still there. Thus this evidence, if such it is, would seem to point to Donovan's death sometime in 1920.

9. Rohan, *Rags*, 106.

10. Rohan, *Rags*, 106-7.

11. Rohan, *Rags*, 107.

12. Rohan, *Rags*, 108; Rand, *Signet*, June 1919, 34-35.

13. Rand, *Signet*, June 1919, 34-35; Rhett, *The History of Fort Sheridan*, 49.

14. Army School of Nursing, Class of 1921, *The Annual*, 225.

15. Rohan, *Rags*, 110-12.

7. FAMILY

1. Seitz, family history, 1.

2. Lorenzo M. Johnson obituary, *New York Times*, November 30, 1904; Seitz, family history, 8, 9.

3. Seitz, family history, 31.

4. Seitz, family history, 33; "Col. Hardenbergh, Pershing War Aide," *New York Times*, February 4, 1949, expressly mentions Rags, "the famous Army mascot."

5. "'Sergeant Rags' a Yellow-Haired Mut." Hardenbergh's acceptance as major is recorded in the *Official Army Register*, July 1, 1921. Washington DC: War Department, Document 1072, Adjutant General's Office, 811.

6. Rhett, *The History of Fort Sheridan*, 48-49.

7. Rohan, *Rags*, 113-14.

8. Rohan, *Rags*, 114.

9. Rohan, *Rags*, 116.

10. Rohan, *Rags*, 118.

11. "'Sergeant Rags' a Yellow-Haired Mut."

12. Rohan, *Rags*, 119-20.

13. Rohan, *Rags*, 120.

8. GOVERNORS ISLAND

1. Rohan, *Rags*, 136.
2. Rohan, *Rags*, 122–23.
3. "Fort Benning"; Historic American Buildings Survey, HABS GA-2392-B, lcweb2.loc.gov/pnp/habshaer/ga/ga0900/ga0983/data/ga0983data .pdf.
4. "'Sergeant Rags' a Yellow-Haired Mut."
5. Rohan, *Rags*, 125.
6. Rohan, *Rags*, 126.
7. Rohan, *Rags*, 126.
8. Beers, *Prevention of Cruelty*, 43–45.
9. "'Sergeant Rags' a Yellow-Haired Mut."
10. Rohan, *Rags*, 128.
11. "Family Tree"; photograph of Sue and Rags on the porch of the Fort Jay residence, Butkus Collection; photo of Rags with sign made for the Long Island Kennel Club Dog Show, 1925, Seitz Collection.
12. Anne Buttenwieser in *Governors Island* (184–85) lists some of the many dogs known to have lived on the military base.
13. Rohan, *Rags*, 138.
14. Rohan, *Rags*, 138.
15. Rohan, *Rags*, 143.
16. Rohan, *Rags*, 144–45.
17. Rohan, *Rags*, 146.
18. Rohan, *Rags*, 146.
19. Rohan, *Rags*, 147; "'Sergeant Rags' a Yellow-Haired Mut"; "World War I Mascot." The men of the Eighteenth did truly care about Rags; a generation later, a historian searching through the regiment's scrapbook found Rags's obituary pasted prominently on one of its pages.
20. Rohan, *Rags*, 148–50.
21. Rohan, *Rags*, 152–53. By 1930 Jack Rohan was living at 38 West 10th Street, Manhattan, a street of old brownstones, working as a newspaper editor. In the mid-1920s he could well have been employed with the Information Service. See image 227.0, roll 1558, p. 2A, census place Manhattan, enumeration district 0245, 1930, Family History Library microfilm 234129.3.
22. Rohan, *Rags*, 153.

9. FAME

1. Rohan, *Rags*, 158.
2. Rohan, *Rags*, 160.
3. "'Sergeant Rags' a Yellow-Haired Mut."
4. Dalziel quoted in Derr, *A Dog's History*, 236.

5. Farthing, *No Dog Left Behind*, 183; Farthing, *Wylie*, 50–51. Farthing refers to Hadiths 3:515, 4:541, and 4:4542. For Wylie's story, see "Afghan Stray Wylie Goes from Dog Fighting to Crufts." ITV, March 7, 2014. http://www.itv.com/news/2014-03-07/afghan-stray-wylie-goes-from-dog-fighting-to-crufts/; see also the Nowzad website: http://www.nowzad.com/about/. In 2010 two of Farthing's rescues, the eponymous Nowzad and Tali, also made it to the Scruffts finals. Around the same time Wylie was rescued, another Afghan dog, Brin, performed jobs for soldiers at a British base in Helmand province not dissimilar to those Rags offered the men of the First Division in France, including warning troops of incoming shells. With no training, Brin was also able to detect improvised explosive devices. Brin, who was rescued by Nowzad and now lives in Britain with his guardian, Sally Baldwin, was also honored at Crufts (http://dogtime.com/canine-hero-from-afghanistan-nominated-for-crufts-honor.html). It should be pointed out that there is no nation on earth where animals in general or dogs in particular are consistently treated with the kindness most people would consider appropriate, just as even in nations demonized for the actions of a small portion of their citizens there are many people working to rescue and protect animals of all kinds from harm.

6. Sarah Singleton to the author, April 21, 2014.

7. Rohan, *Rags*, 164.

8. "Family Tree." Besides or instead of poodle, Rags may have had a considerable amount of Pyrenean shepherd ancestry. In weight, coat, curling tail, and uncanny ability to quickly learn all the tasks put to him by Donovan and others during his several months of battlefield service, Rags bore many "Pyr shep" traits. See http://www.dogster.com/dog-breeds/Pyrenean_Shepherd.

9. "Family Tree."

10. From photos reproduced in Rohan and from the Butkus and Seitz Collections. In all photographs of this sign, the last line is blocked either by Rags or by the men standing around him, making it impossible to know what it actually said. However, it is possible it reads something like, "Rags, mascot of the First Division."

11. "Family Tree."

12. Hickman was awarded the Mexican Interior Service Medal (for the first Battle of Agua Prieta, 1911), the Victory Medal "with five bars and three silver stars," the Purple Heart, the Silver Star, the Verdun Medal (French), and the First Division Medal for taking part in all engagements. Clippings undated, Kemmerer Collection.

13. George E. Hickman to sister, May 11, 1919, Kemmerer Collection.

14. U.S. Census 1920, U.S. Census 1930, Ancestry.com; undated clippings, Kemmerer Collection, Hickman Family Records. George Hickman died in New Orleans, Louisiana, on New Year's Day 1962.

15. "Family Tree."
16. Rohan, *Rags*, 169. Sergeant Stubby had also been entered in, and temporarily excluded from, a dog show in Boston, only for the judges to overrule the club's members and award Stubby a "gold hero medal" to add to all the others pinned to his jacket; see Derr, *A Dog's History*, 260.
17. "Rags Is Genial Host to Devil Dogs' Dog," *New York Times*, March 28, 1927; "Army and Marine Mascots Meet," *Waterloo (in) Press*, April 7, 1927; "Mascot Mourns Mascot," undated clipping, Seitz Collection.
18. "Family Tree."
19. Rohan, *Rags*, 170.
20. "$25 Sent to 'Rags,' A.E.F. Hero," undated clipping, Seitz Collection.
21. "Rags, Barred from Dog Show, to Have a Show All His Own," *New York Times*, October 16, 1925; "War Dog Enters Show Where Red Blood Counts," *New York Herald Tribune*, October 1925.
22. Rohan, *Rags*, 171.
23. Bausum, *Sergeant Stubby*, 187–89.
24. "Army Enters 'Rags.'"
25. New York Junior League, "Our Story: 1911–1929," https://www.nyjl.org/?nd=about_our_stry_1911_1929; *National Humane Review* (Albany NY), August 1917, 143–44, http://babel.hathitrust.org/cgi/pt?id=chi.105129478;view=1up;seq=156.
26. "Army Enters 'Rags.'" An interesting bit of trivia: the Waldorf Astoria Hotel that Rags knew, razed in 1929 to build the Empire State Building, was designed by Henry Janeway Hardenbergh, a cousin of Maj. Raymond W. Hardenbergh.
27. "First Division Celebrates; Battles Re-enacted on Anniversary of Firing of First Shot in War," *New York Times*, October 25, 1925.
28. "First Division Celebrates."
29. Rohan, *Rags*, 181–82.
30. Rohan, *Rags*, 183.
31. "War Dog in Town: Rags Is at Fort Hamilton for Divisional Reunion," 1929. Butkus Collection.
32. Rohan, *Rags*, 211.
33. "Army Wants Its Lost Dog!" November 1, 1929, Butkus Collection.
34. Rohan, *Rags*, 213–15; "Rags Won't Be Back at Fort Until Next Month," undated clipping (ca. 1930), Seitz Collection.
35. "Fightin' First Goes over Top for Rags," *New York Daily News*, November 1, 1929. According to other reports, Summerall was not even at Fort Hamilton by the date of Rags's disappearance.
36. "Rags AWOL: First Division's Dog Mascot Lost, Strayed or Stolen," undated clipping, Butkus Collection.

37. Bradshaw, *Dog Sense*, 171.

38. "1st Sees Its Flag Decorated: Battle Streamers for Heroism Presented by Gen. Summerall at Fort Hamilton Fete," *New York Times*, November 3, 1929.

39. Rohan, *Rags*, 238–39.

40. Rohan, *Rags*, 186.

41. Cooling, "Dwight D. Eisenhower," 25.

42. Rohan states that one of the policemen reported the incident between Pershing and Rags to an army sergeant, who then passed it along the chain (*Rags*, 195).

43. Perry, *Pershing*, 200–201.

44. Rohan, *Rags*, 191–95.

45. Rohan, *Rags*, 204.

46. Rohan, *Rags*, 206.

47. Boone, *Kinship*, 31–32; Rohan, *Rags*, 208.

10. OLD WARRIOR

1. Derr, *A Dog's History*, 275.

2. Orlean, *Rin Tin Tin*, 66; Beers, *Prevention of Cruelty*, 104.

3. "Rags Lives to See Biography Sent to British War Museum," *Manitowoc (WI) Herald-News*, November 17, 1930.

4. "Rags Lives to See Biography."

5. "Rags Lives to See Biography."

6. "Rags Lives to See Biography."

7. "Immortality This Dog's Fate," undated clipping, Seitz Collection; title page of Rohan, *Rags*, 1930, collection of the Imperial War Museum, London, acc. no. 13619.

8. Steel, *Angel in Top Hat*, 64–65.

9. "Lone Anti-vivisectionist: Mrs. Diana Belais Does Battle against Three Surgeons at a Woman's Club," *New York Times*, April 15, 1908.

10. Lorena Hickock, "Dog Hero of War Is Bored as He Gets New Medal," *Joplin Globe*, January 10, 1931, 1.

11. Hickock, "Dog Hero of War."

12. Hickock, "Dog Hero of War."

13. Masson, *Dogs Never Lie*, 115–16.

14. "Canine War Hero," *Freeport (IL) Journal-Standard*, January 15, 1934.

15. "Governors Island Gains 8-8 Tie with New York A.C.'s Quartet," *New York Times*, May 13, 1935.

11. THE DOG THAT HAD A SOUL

1. Maryland Inventory of Historic Properties, form M: 27-17 for Aspin Hill Pet Cemetery, Maryland Historical Trust, Crownsville, Maryland. A later and

once-famous Maryland pet cemetery is Rosa Bonheur Memorial Park, located in Elkridge near Baltimore. Named for Bonheur (1822–99), the French painter whose animal portraits gave personality and dignity to what most people of her day considered mere beasts of burden, Rosa Bonheur Memorial Park was founded in 1935. Among its interments is Gypsy Queen, the mare ridden through all forty-eight states (1925–27) by World War I veteran Frank Heath; Corporal Rex Ahlbin, a World War II Marine Corps combat dog; and Carlo, who at age twenty-seven was even older than Rags at the time of his death.

2. "50 Washington Lovers of Animals Pay Tribute at Last Resting Place of Their Departed Pets," undated clipping, Butkus Collection.

3. Harrison, *Descendants*, 2679–80.

4. For the Ball connection, see Ancestry.com, *The Leland Family of Virginia et al. 2014*, http://trees.ancestry.com/tree/67052555/person/40163630367?ssrc=&ml_rpos=12; for the Madison connection, see Ancestry.com, *Reed Family Tree*, http://trees.ancestry.com/tree/25672050/person/2015561500/family/pedigree/.

5. Vaughan, *Encyclopedia*, 50.

6. 1920 Census, Charles Harris, Maryland, image 181, roll T625-71, p. 4B, enumeration district 46, Ancestry.com.

7. Quoting Maryland Inventory of Historic Properties form M: 27-17, 2; Long Island reference from undated newspaper clipping, "Rags Won't Be Back."

8. Quoting Maryland Inventory of Historic Properties, form M: 27-17, 2.

9. Quoted in Maryland Inventory of Historic Properties, form M: 27-17, 3. Aspin Hill's owner, Montgomery County Humane Society, owns the original brochure.

10. Quoting Maryland Inventory of Historic Properties, form M: 27-17, 3; 1930 United States Census.

11. "50 Washington Lovers of Animals."

12. For Mickey's mausoleum, see Robert M. Andrews, "FBI Director Was Hard on Criminals, Soft on Dogs," Associated Press, July 18, 1990; Maryland Inventory of Historic Properties, form M: 27-17, 3; Patric, "Roads from Washington," 41.

13. "50 Washington Lovers of Animals."

14. As quoted in Maryland Inventory of Historic Properties, form M: 27-17, 2.

15. 1940 United States Census, in which Richard Birney gives his years of education and is not described as a veterinarian.

16. Patric, "Roads from Washington," 41.

17. Raymond W. Hardenbergh to C. V. Allan, March 19, 1936, Butkus Collection.

18. Hardenbergh to Allan, March 19, 1936.

19. Minna Irving to Raymond W. Hardenbergh, March 12, 1936, Butkus Collection.

20. "Flag on Dog's Grave Starts Battle," undated clipping, Butkus Collection.
21. Jack Rohan to Raymond W. Hardenbergh, March 23, 1936, Butkus Collection.
22. Jack Rohan to Raymond W. Hardenbergh, March 23, 1936, Butkus Collection.
23. "Rags, Dog Veteran of War."
24. Quote from Kenji Onozawa to Raymond W. Hardenbergh, undated; see also Raymond W. Hardenbergh to Kenji Onozawa, March 31, 1936, both in Butkus Collection. In 1936 Onozawa was living at 346 Central Street in Wichendon, Massachusetts, the home of Mrs. Campanole's parents, Mr. and Mrs. Ernest Wood. See *Fitchburg Sentinel*, December 3, 1929, 14.
25. Schnurmacher quoted in "A Bonus for Dog Veterans," *New York Times*, June 19, 1936. Bobby was a "little brown dog" serving with his master, Capt. D. C. Harris, of Macon, Georgia, seven years in the National Guard. He was made a lieutenant as a practical joke. In 1927, long after Rags had lived there, Bobby was the pet of Fort Benning, Georgia. See "Little Dog Rates Salute; He's 'Lieutenant Bobby,'" *Ludington Daily News*, August 13, 1930. Around the same time Rags was at Fort Benning, there was a resident mascot, a stray dog named Calculator for his habit, when hungry, of pretending to be lame in one foot (he put down three and carried one). Calculator was beloved by the Fort Benning men, but somebody poisoned him in August 1923. He is buried at Fort Benning; his stone monument has been moved to the grounds of the National Infantry Museum in Columbus, Georgia.
26. Schnurmacher quoted in "A Bonus for Dog Veterans."
27. A. P. Terhune, "War Hero Is 'Oldest Inhabitant,'" *Ogden Standard-Examiner*, October 11, 1936.
28. Raymond W. Hardenbergh to Minna Irving, March 31, 1936, Butkus Collection.
29. Irving, poem, undated, Butkus Collection.
30. Raymond W. Hardenbergh to C. V. Allen, March 25, 1936, Butkus Collection.
31. "Flag on Dog's Grave."
32. Metcalf's Great War draft registration: roll 1993027, Wood County, West Virginia; his World War II draft registration, giving physical characteristics: National Records and Archives Administration (NARA), series M1939; NARA series title, World War II Draft Cards (Fourth Registration) for the State of Maryland; Archival Research Catalog (ARC) no. 563727; ARC title, Fourth Registration Draft Cards, 04/27/1942–04/27/1942; creator, Selective Service System; Maryland State Headquarters (1940–1947); RG 147; Records of the Selective Service System, 1926–1975, National Archives at St. Louis, St. Louis, Missouri. Ironically, when Metcalf died in 1985, nobody bothered to put his year of death on his stone, which bears a tentative "19——." See Find-a-Grave, http://www.findagrave.com/cgi-bin/fg.cgi?page=gr&GRid=80161505.

33. "Owner of Cemetery for Dogs Denies 'Desecration' of Flag," *Washington Post*, Mary 26, 1937. The DAR does not appear to have taken Metcalf's appeal seriously.
34. "Use of Flags on Graves of Dogs Is Hit by Nearby Legion Post," undated clipping, Butkus Collection; *Stars and Stripes* article quoted in Bausum, *Sergeant Stubby*, 169.
35. "Owner of Cemetery for Dogs."
36. "Flag on Dog's Grave."
37. Thurston quoted in "War Dog Given a Hero's Funeral," *Daily News*, February 21, 2001," and email to the author, September 2, 2014.
38. "Flags and Dog's Graves," undated clipping, Butkus Collection.

12. WAR HERO

1. Gail Patten, email to author, May 22, 2014.
2. Another son of Helen and John Seitz, diplomat Raymond G. H. Seitz, was United States ambassador to the Court of St. James from 1991 to 1994. Ambassador Seitz, too, inherited his share of Hardenbergh Rags memorabilia. Seitz Family history, including family anecdotes about Rags. Seitz Collection.
3. Altschul, "My 2-Cents-Worth," *Web of Life*, November 25, 2006, http://web oflife.wordpress.com/2006/11/. b j Altschul died on May 31, 2014, in Silver Spring, Maryland. Among her many professional affiliations prior to working for the Montgomery County Humane Society (http://mchumane .org/), b j had served as assistant professor and adjunct professor at American University in Washington DC, at the University of Maryland, University of Richmond, Virginia, and Old Dominion University in Norfolk, Virginia. She was faculty advisor to the student division of the Public Relations Student Society of America, served on the board of the District of Columbia Science Writers Association, and was chair of the Virginia State Agency Public Affairs Association. She volunteered for Earthwatch Institute, the American Cancer Society, and Big Brothers / Big Sisters and for her public relations work earned many awards (obituary, *Washington Post*, May 31, 2014).
4. Elizabeth Waibel, "Public to Vote on Grant Money for Historic Preservation in Montgomery County," *Gaithersburg (MD) Gazette*, April 29, 2013.
5. Silverman, *Defending Animal Rights*, 40.
6. Silverman, *Defending Animal Rights*, 41.
7. Bart Barnes, "Dorothy M. Shapiro, Philanthropist Who Oversaw Family's Trust, Dies at 90," *Washington Post*, June 12, 2012.
8. Howard Rosenberg, "Fighting Tooth and Claw: Ingrid Newkirks's Combative Style and Headline-Grabbing Stunts Have Shaken Up the Animal-Rights Movement," *Los Angeles Times*, March 22, 1992; Ingrid Newkirk to author, September 6, 2014.

9. Cameron W. Barr, "Pet Owners Grieving All Over Again," *Washington Post*, January 11, 2005.
10. Mary Pemberton, "Abused Critters Find Safety, Respect," *Los Angeles Times*, August 29, 1993; Newkirk to author.
11. Barnes, "Dorothy M. Shapiro."
12. Effie Bathen, "State Questions Charitable Status of Pet Cemetery," *Gaithersburg (MD) Gazette*, February 18, 2004.
13. Barr, "Pet Owners Grieving."
14. Melissa J. Brachfeld, "A New Life for Aspin Hill Pet Cemetery," *Gaithersburg (MD) Gazette*, May 28, 2008.
15. Margie Hyslop, "Humane Society Struggles to Maintain Pet Cemetery," *Gaithersburg (MD) Gazette*, July 1, 2009.
16. Mimi Liu and Margie Hyslop, "Montgomery County Planning Board Approves Zoning Change Lifting Restrictions on Historic Resource Sites," *Gaithersburg (MD) Gazette*, June 8, 2011.

BIBLIOGRAPHY

ARCHIVAL SOURCES

Jay and Judy Butkus Collection. Burtonsville, Maryland.

Family History Library. Salt Lake City, Utah.

Hickman Family Records. San Antonio, Texas.

Imperial War Museum. London.

Claudia Kemmerer Collection. San Antonio, Texas.

Maryland Historical Trust. Crownsville, Maryland.

Montgomery County Humane Society Archives.

National Archives at St. Louis. St. Louis, Missouri.

Seitz Collection. Orford, New Hampshire.

PUBLISHED SOURCES

Army School of Nursing, Class of 1921. *The Annual*. https://archive.org/details
    /ArmyNursingAnnual1921.

Ascher-Walsh, Rebecca. *Devoted: 38 Extraordinary Tales of Love, Loyalty, and Life
    with Dogs*. Washington DC: National Geographic Society, 2013.

Bausum, Ann. *Sergeant Stubby: How a Stray Dog and His Best Friend Helped Win
    World War I and Stole the Heart of a Nation*. Washington DC: National Geo-
    graphic Books, 2014.

Baynes, Ernest Harold. *Animal Heroes of the Great War*. New York: Macmillan,
    1925.

Baynes, Ernest Harold, and Louis Agassiz Fuentes. *The Book of Dogs*. Washington
    DC: National Geographic Society, 1919.

Beers, Diane L. *For the Prevention of Cruelty: The History and Legacy of Animal
    Rights Activism in the United States*. Athens: Ohio University Press, 2006.

Bekoff, Marc. *The Emotional Lives of Animals: A Leading Scientist Explores Animal
    Joy, Sorrow, and Empathy—and Why They Matter*. Novato CA: New World
    Library, 2007.

Boone, J. Allen. *Kinship with All Life*. New York: Harper & Brothers, 1954.

Bradshaw, John. Dog Sense: How the New Science of Dog Behavior Can Make
    You a Better Friend to Your Pet. New York: Basic Books, 2011.

Buttenweiser, Ann L. *Governors Island: The Jewel of New York Harbor*. Syracuse NY: Syracuse University Press, 2009.

Campsie, Philippa. "Parisian Fields: Paris in the First World War." October 27, 2013. http://parisianfields.wordpress.com/2013/10/27/paris-in-the-first-world-war/.

Clark, George. *The American Expeditionary Force in World War I: A Statistical History*. Jefferson NC: McFarland & Company, 2013.

Clodfelter, Michael. *The Lost Battalion and the Meuse-Argonne, 1918: America's Deadliest Battle*. Jefferson NC: McFarland & Company, 2007.

Cochrane, Raymond C. *Gas Warfare in World War I: The 1st Division in the Meuse-Argonne, 1–12 October 1918*. Washington DC: U.S. Army Chemical Corps Historical Office, Office of the Chief Chemical Officer, 1957.

Coolidge, John Gardner. *A War Diary in Paris 1914–1917*. Cambridge MA: Riverside Press, 1931.

Cooling, Dr. Benjamin F., III. "Dwight D. Eisenhower at the Army War College, 1927–1928." *Parameters: The Journal of the U.S. Army War College* 5, no. 1 (1975) (Carlisle PA).

Cooper, Jilly. *Animals in War*. London: Corgi Books / Random House, 2000.

———. *Intelligent & Loyal: A Celebration of the Mongrel*. London: Eyre Methuen, 1981.

Coren, Stanley. *The Pawprints of History: Dogs and the Course of Human Events*. New York: Free Press / Simon & Schuster, 2002.

———. *What Do Dogs Know?* New York: Free Press / Simon & Schuster, 1997.

Derr, Mark. *A Dog's History of America: How Our Best Friend Explored, Conquered, and Settled a Continent*. New York: North Point Press, 2004.

Dowling, Mike. *Sergeant Rex: The Unbreakable Bond between a Marine and His Military Working Dog*. New York: Simon & Schuster, 2011.

Ellis, John. *Eye-Deep in Hell: Trench Warfare in World War I*. Baltimore: Johns Hopkins University Press, 1989.

Farthing, Pen. *No Place like Home: A New Beginning with the Dogs of Afghanistan*. London: Ebury Press, 2010.

———. *One Dog at a Time*. London: Ebury Press, 2009.

———. *Wylie: The Brave Street Dog Who Never Gave Up*. London: Hodder & Stoughton, 2014.

"Fort Benning." *New Georgia Encyclopedia*, edited by Beryl I. Diamond and NGE Staff, Georgia State University, 2003/2013. http://www.georgiaencyclopedia.org/articles/government-politics/fort-benning.

Freidel, Frank. *Over There: The Story of America's First Great Overseas Crusade*. Boston: Little, Brown, 1964.

Glen, Susan L. *Images of America: Governors Island*. Charleston: Arcadia Publishing, 2006.

Goodavage, Maria. *Soldier Dogs: The Untold Story of America's Canine Heroes*. New York: New American Library, 2012.

Harrison, Bruce. *Descendants of Lady Joan Beaufort of Beaufort Castle*. Kamuela HI: Millisecond Publishing Co., 2009.

Horowitz, Alexandra. *Inside of a Dog: What Dogs See, Smell, and Know*. New York: Scribner, 2009.

Jaffin, Maj. Jonathan H. "Medical Support for the American Expeditionary Forces in France during the First World War." MA thesis, 1991. U.S. Army Command and Staff College, Fort Leavenworth KS. http://history.amedd.army.mil/booksdocs/wwi/Jaffin/.

Johnson, Douglas, and Madeleine Johnson. *The Age of Illusion: Art and Politics in France, 1918-1940*. New York: Rizzoli, 1987.

Laurence, Alison G. "Patriot, Pet, and Pest: America Debates the Dog's Worth during World War I." MA thesis, Brown University, 2011. scholarworks.uno.edu/cgi/viewcontent.cgi?article=2655&context=td.

Leffingwell, Albert. *Vivisection in America*. New York: Macmillan, 1894.

Lemish, Michael G. *War Dogs: A History of Loyalty and Heroism*. Washington DC: Potomac Books, 2008.

Le Naour, Jean-Yves. *The Living Unknown Soldier: A Story of Grief and the Great War*. Translated by Penny Allen. New York: Metropolitan Books / Henry Holt, 2004.

Lengel, Edward G. *To Conquer Hell: The Meuse-Argonne, 1918, the Epic Battle That Ended the First World War*. New York: Henry Holt & Company, 2008.

Liggett, Maj. Gen. Hunter. *A.E.F.: Ten Years Ago in France*. New York: Dodd, Mead & Company, 1927.

Link, Arthur S. "The Enigma of Woodrow Wilson." *American Mercury*, September 1947.

Lubow, Robert E. *The War Animals: The Training and Use of Animals as Weapons of War*. New York: Doubleday & Company, 1977.

"Lynbrook Dog Won Fame in Army." World War I veterans' service data and photographs, 1917-1938. Series A0412-78, box 13, folder 2. Division of Archives and History, Education Department, New York State Archives. http://iarchives.nysed.gov/vdms/viewImageData.jsp?id=157923&language=english.

MacDonogh, Katharine. *Reigning Cats and Dogs: A History of Pets at Court since the Renaissance*. New York: St. Martin's Press, 1999.

Marshall, Gen. George C. *Memoirs of My Services in the World War 1917-1918*. Boston: Houghton Mifflin, 1976.

Masson, Jeffrey. *Dogs Never Lie about Love*. New York: Vintage, 1998.

Mead, Gary. *The Doughboys: America and the First World War*. New York: Overlook Press, 2000.

Nelson, James Carl. *Five Lieutenants: The Heartbreaking Story of Five Harvard Men Who Led America to Victory in World War I*. New York: St. Martin's Press, 2012.

Officers of the Eighty-Second Division. *Official History of 82nd Division, American Expeditionary Forces, 1917–1919*. Indianapolis: Bobbs-Merrill Company, 1919.

Orlean, Susan. *Rin Tin Tin: The Life and the Legend*. New York: Simon & Schuster, 2011.

Orsi, Maj. Douglas J. "The Effectiveness of the U.S. Army Signal Corps in Support of the American Expeditionary Force Division and Below Maneuver Units during World War I." MA thesis, U.S. Army Command and Staff College, 2001. Fort Leavenworth KS. www.dtic.mil/dtic/tr/fulltext/u2/a396881.pdf.

Page, Jake. *Dogs: A Natural History*. New York: HarperCollins, 2007.

Patric, John. "Roads from Washington." *National Geographic*, July 1938.

Perry, John. *Pershing: Commander of the Great War*. New York: Thomas Nelson / HarperCollins, 2011.

Pershing, Gen. John J. *My Experiences in the First World War*. New York: Da Capo Press, 1995.

Peterson, Dale. *The Moral Lives of Animals*. New York: Bloomsbury, 2011.

Rand, Frank Prentice, ed. *Signet*, June 1919. Phi Sigma Kappa Fraternity, North Amherst MA.

Rearick, Charles. *Pleasures of the Belle Epoque: Entertainment & Festivity in Turn-of-the-Century France*. New Haven: Yale University Press, 1985.

Regimental Adjutant, Twenty-Sixth Infantry. *The Twenty-Sixth Infantry in France*. Montabaur-Frankfurt: Martin Flock & Co., 1919.

Remington, Frederic. *Crooked Trails*. New York: Harper & Brothers, 1898.

Rhett, Col. John T. *The History of Fort Sheridan, Illinois*. Lake County Museum of History, Wadsworth IL.

Richardson, Lt. Col. E. H. *British War Dogs: Their Training and Psychology*. London: Skeffington & Son, 1920.

Rogak, Lisa. *The Dogs of War: The Courage, Love, and Loyalty of Military Working Dogs*. New York: St. Martin's Press, 2011.

Rohan, Jack. *Rags: The Story of a Dog Who Went to War*. New York: Grosset & Dunlap, 1930.

Shipley, Capt. Thomas. *The History of the A.E.F.* New York: George H. Doran Company, 1920.

Silverman, B. P. Robert. *Defending Animal Rights Is the Right Thing to Do*. New York: S.P.I. Books / Shapolsky Publishers, 1991.

Smith, Guy Vernon. *The Bishop of London's Visit to the Front*. London: Longmans and Green, 1915.

Society of the First Division. *History of the First Division during the World War, 1917–1919*. Philadelphia: John C. Winston Company, 1922.

Steel, Zulma. *Angel in Top Hat*. New York: Harper & Brothers, 1942.

Summerall, Gen. Charles Pelot. *The Way of Duty, Honor, Country: The Memoir of Charles Pelot Summerall*, ed. Timothy K. Nenninger. Lexington: University Press of Kentucky, 2010.

United States Army, Seventh Field Artillery Regiment. *History of the Seventh Field Artillery (First Division, A.E.F.): World War, 1917–1919*. New York: J. J. Little and Ives, 1929.

Van Emden, Richard. *Tommy's Ark: Soldiers and Their Animals in the Great War*. New York: Bloomsbury, 2010.

Vaughan, Stephen L., ed. *Encyclopedia of American Journalism*. New York: Routledge, Taylor & Francis, 2008.

von Kreisler, Kristin. *The Compassion of Animals: True Stories of Animal Courage and Kindness*. New York: Prima Publishing, 1997.

———. *For Bea: The Story of the Beagle Who Changed My Life*. New York: Jeremy P. Tarcher / Putnam, 2003.

Woollcott, Alexander. *Verdun Belle and Some Others*. New York: Grosset & Dunlap, 1928.

Wynne, William A. *Yorkie Doodle Dandy: A Memoir*. Denver: Top Dog Enterprises, 1996.

Young, Bailey K. "Archaeology in an Urban Setting: Excavations at Saint-Pierre-de-Montmartre, Paris, 1975–1977." *Journal of Field Archaeology* 5, no. 3 (Autumn 1978).

INDEX

OTHER WORKS BY GRANT HAYTER-MENZIES

*Charlotte Greenwood: The Life and Career of
the Comic Star of Vaudeville, Radio and Film*

Imperial Masquerade: The Legend of Princess Der Ling

Mrs. Ziegfeld: The Public and Private Lives of Billie Burke

*The Empress and Mrs. Conger: The Uncommon
Friendship of Two Women and Two Worlds*

Shadow Woman: The Extraordinary Career of Pauline Benton

Lillian Carter: A Compassionate Life